In the Nick of Time

Films of this moment and others

by Jonathan Price

dolcefarniente

Fair Oaks, California

In the Nick of Time: Films of this moment and others
by Jonathan Price

Published under the imprint

dolcefarniente

Fair Oaks, California

ISBN 978-0-692-16537-9

Edited, indexed, & formatted for publication by Morris Dean
Cover design by Janice Cataldi-Price & Morris Dean

Contents

In the Nick of Time

Films of this moment and others

Introduction

I found it at the Movies:
Not twelve years a slave, but six years an occasional film reviewer

AS JOHN BARTH once remarked, it's always dangerous to include an allusion in a title, because it almost inevitably reminds the reader of a writer better than you (in this case, Pauline Kael). I guess that should bother me, but it didn't bother Hemingway much when he alluded to Ecclesiastes in *The Sun Also Rises*. Not that I include myself in this particular company, but then so far as I know neither Hemingway nor Ecclesiastes wrote film reviews.

This collection of reviews, written over the last six years, is not necessarily of the best films in those years, certainly not of the worst. If they're not all worth seeing again, some are worth seeing at least once and lingering over, thinking about. That is what I have tried to do, hoping you will occasionally do some of the same with these or others. With the exceptions of the most recent reviews, very few of these films are now available in movie theaters. So this collection may point you to films you've missed or films you might want to see on a smaller screen. I hope that what I'm offering you is useful for that ever-harassed and confused search for evening or weekend home entertainment.

It's inevitable that many (perhaps all) of my prejudices about film, reviewing, life, literature, and the kitchen sink are on parade in these reviews, especially to those who know me well. But it might be helpful to the reader to point some of these out in advance, so that you're forewarned, or perhaps even comfortable when you encounter them in the following pages.

Films are an art form. I didn't use to believe this, growing up and being pretty conventional in my social and artistic judgments and favoring the traditional art forms of the time—classical music, painting, sculpture, and literature. But I certainly have always enjoyed watching films, and have continued to do so, trying to keep to a steady addictive diet of two a week. In cities where more variety is available, I indulge more frequently.

In college I began to learn, along with the advent of the French *nouvelle vague*, that films weren't just popular, demotic entertainment, but were also artistically conceived, of some sophistication, and to be admired and studied, frequently, for these qualities. It's not such a surprise that a dedicated group of workers with varied backgrounds and striving for some kind of excellence or prominence, should frequently achieve artistic merit—whether there are 20 or, more lately, 1,000 of them, as we might note in the increasingly longer credit sequences that accompany contemporary films. Such an artistic medium is therefore not merely or not only entertainment, a frivolous activity to while away an afternoon or evening, or to emulate its 40-foot high actors in various gestures; but is something to be thought about, responded to, studied, even seen again for the purposes of greater enjoyment and analysis. And thus there is always more to a film than first meets the eye or mind. Films are part of a particular culture and are almost inevitably and often quite self-consciously comments on that culture—political, personal, historic, speculative, and often joyous statements. It's probable that you already believe some of this, or you wouldn't have picked up this book.

It's also a misconception to think of a film as a reproduction of a book or—in many cases—a novel, though this is a conventional critical conundrum: how true is the film to the book? This kind of thinking can only, for the most part, lead astray those of us who love films. As I used to say to my film students (for I was, alas, periodically a professor who taught film courses), "the only way to make a film absolutely true to a book would be to place a camera in front of a text and slowly turn the pages." This would probably make for a unique cinematic experience, but a fairly empty auditorium, though I am compelled to remind the reader, at least momentarily, of Andy Warhol's experimental film *Empire*, which placed a camera in front of the Empire State Building and let it run for hours. A climactic moment came when a pigeon passed by.

Certain genres and tendencies in film tend to annoy me, and I rant against them—often unfairly. One of these is the tendency to offer endless remakes or sequels of very successful or popular films. Occasionally this may be profitable or even artistically powerful, as in *Godfather II* (I am moved to point out that the second film was conceived at the same time and "from" the same novel, and with many of the same actors, as the first film, and shot simultaneously, only cut and distributed later). The pattern would seem to bely the originality and creativity that are the hallmark of any art form. Perhaps an attentive and critical reader will point out that numerous artistic renderings of Madonna and Child never sapped the supply nor the successive enjoyment of viewers. Some others might say, didn't *The Godfather* come from a book, and wasn't it successful? I would suggest to them that they read Mario Puzo's novel carefully, then compare it to Coppola's two films, scene by scene, paying attention not only to plot but also to camera angle, editing, and dialogue: and recognize how much has been omitted or transformed from the "source."

Also annoying to me are dystopic end-of-the-world films, which, despite their seeming creativity and strangeness, often seem overdetermined by sameness, repetition, predictability. These films seem typically, almost formulaically, to display an anti-humanity and coldness that I find distasteful. Luckily, *The World's End*, here reviewed, doesn't appear to share these qualities. But I have also reviewed and commented on several other dystopic films; they come along quite frequently.

I don't like the star system, at least as used among reviewers. I find it's a kind of misleading shorthand, certainly for me, and potentially for many others who might go to movies. Why five stars at the most? Why not ten, or twenty? What's really the difference between a four-star film and a three-star film? One of the films I've incorporated here and seriously enjoyed and appreciated when I saw it—*Maudie*—a local critic identified as the very worst film of the year; personally I doubted she'd seen, or at least thought very carefully about *Home Again*, a film I declined to review but that constantly seemed to be searching for a plot, a gimmick, a convincing story to appeal to audiences—this film seemed a far better candidate for worst film of the year; but all that shows films reviews are about differences of opinion; and, as Mark Twain notes, that's why they have horse races. Investigated seriously, I suspect, the stars are simply a reflection of a critic's immediate, personal, biased, particular, and emotional reactions. As are my reviews. I wouldn't want to make a greater claim for them. I certainly wouldn't want the reviews or their judgments to perpetually damn or exalt individual works—as stars and Academy

Awards often tend to do. It's worth remembering that *Citizen Kane*, a film now extremely highly regarded by film critics and historians, in its time (1942) won only one academy award out of nine nominations.

Another warning is a sort of "spoiler alert." Periodically you'll see in these reviews an early warning that I'm about to disclose plot details. For me it's almost impossible to write much coherent or noteworthy about a feature film without disclosing some kind of plot detail. To some extent these reviews are written as preliminary discussions with the reader after she or he may have seen the film: they are intended to provoke discussion, not—like so many reviews—to tell you whether to go out and see the film. So it's almost impossible not to "spoil" a narrative experience for a prospective audience to some extent while discussing the nature of that narrative experience. However, if we think very long about it, we realize the word "spoiler" is a condensed and abbreviated misnomer. It's hard, I think, to "spoil" a film the way, say, a carton of milk is spoiled. If the carton's spoiled, you don't want any of it, not in a glass, not in your coffee, not in your tea, not in a recipe. But if you know one detail—or several—of a film, it remains available to you and enjoyable in so many ways. To use *The Godfather* as a convenient example, presumably because most readers will be familiar with it: knowing that Woltz (the Hollywood producer) will wake up screaming because he has found his favorite horse's head and blood by his feet under his sheets certainly eliminates one of the film's key surprises, but we can still appreciate the scene (and the film): how Coppola leads up to the walls of the Renaissance villa in the early morning, supposedly serene, safe, secure, old World; how at first Woltz doesn't seem to know (nor would a first-time viewer) whether he has been castrated or wounded or something else has happened; and how we recognize the directness, but "restraint," of Don Corleone's approach to a prospective business associate whom he has made an offer he can't refuse. The film has these surprise climaxes, but it also offers us a portrait of a family business, a slice of American life, an implicit critique of the American dream and perhaps of capitalism/idealism as well.

Having said so much negative, I feel inclined to emphasize the overwhelmingly positive side of cinema, of going out to a film, of thinking about films. It's a childlike experience and it offers many simple joys.

Don't think that because I was once an English professor who occasionally taught films that I claim any special expertise in this field. Everyone is his or her own expert and judge of a film—to me this is one of the attractions of the supposed disciplines of literary and film criticism: even "non-experts" actually have talent, qualification, and valuable points of view. If you like the movie, or it speaks to you, that is virtually unassailable. What I have tried to offer here are comments, reflections, and suggestions about films you may have seen or may have missed over the last few years. Perhaps now they are worth reconsidering on a dull or otherwise uneventful evening

Originally, this text was organized chronologically, in the order these essays/reviews were written and frequently published in my friend Moristotle's blog, "Moristotle & Co." But chronology seems a fairly useless organizational strategy now, and I have not gone back and tried to update everything to 2018; my original references to time stand as they were at the time of original publication to give the book reader some sense of occasional film reviews written at particular times, written over the course of several years. For this collection I have tried to arrange the reviews into recognizable categories. Some are movie genres; but some defy ready labeling—films of the past and the future, and the present moment. The past and the future may not seem like very promising categories, but they subsume a major part of our film imaginings, in Westerns, war films, histories; science fiction films, dystopias. Films that don't fit either of these two categories might be called films of the present moment, or to retrofit Thoreau, films "in the very nick of time." These are films that at first glance may not seem very remarkable, but they attempt to tell us or examine how we live now.

Of course, many films could arguably fit into several categories at once, or one could complain that a given film is placed in the wrong category or genre. Perhaps this would be true of many or most forms of categorization: for me, and I hope for you, it's a useful or productive way to think or re-think about how these films fit into our culture and our lives. Like so many categorization strategies, it's not meant to be all-inclusive. In addition to those three main groupings (past, future, present moment),

8

there are several leftovers, or et ceteras or miscellanies: films about art, film collection reviews, foreign films, the transcendent.

Films about the past, or "facts" (an increasing development strategy, I feel, for recent films), or history seem to satisfy a deep American need for nostalgia, but also for understanding our origins. Initially, one aspect of the past and of history has been War. And there have been many films about war, and especially wars we have fought in, though only a few are reviewed here. As one war participant reputedly said, "only the dead have seen the end of war," and probably we viewers have not seen the end of war or war films, particularly those devoted to the Second World War.

Despite the fact that we began as a revolutionary culture, changing the future, the future so many of these future films point to is almost inevitably dystopic, dark.

Sometimes the films that most touch a nerve or speak deeply to us are those that don't seem to be about anything remarkable but are set in the present of what all of us cope with, the everyday for everybody.

The section of film collections encompasses a few multi-film reviews, usually presented as comparisons (naturally one could classify the films considered in one of the previous categories). Perhaps, in retrospect, here are two films worth reconsidering: *Locke* and *The Rover* (from chapter 21), with bravura performances by unusual actors, Tom Hardy and Guy Pearce. *The Rover* is perhaps remarkable for being a film that might be included in two of the categories I've already mentioned—the past and the future. It's set visually and structurally in a near-Western, iconized environment and involves a Western-like quest: but its time period is that of a dystopic future, and for me it seemed to transcend many of the expected tropes and patterns of dystopic films.

Yet another section includes "perhaps" foreign films. Of course, many foreign films are produced, but fewer these days seem to make it to American shores. The three films treated here challenge us with some reconsiderations of our own viewpoints.

And finally, there is only one film in the category of the transcendent, though certainly that label claims too much. Still, *Life of Pi*, without necessarily being a great film, seems to deserve a category all by itself.

The Past (History)

1. A Tale of Two Captains, an Asymmetrical Conflict: *Captain Phillips*

THE 2013 FILM *Captain Phillips* (directed by Paul Greengrass and starring Tom Hanks) is the story of two captains, but its title tells us nothing of the story, for most of us already know it, whether from reading the papers or seeing the previews, where everyman Hanks-Phillips eventually succeeds in defeating Somali pirates who are trying to take over his ship. Or so it would seem.

Hanks, we know, has won Academy Awards for playing two characters who don't quite seem like heroes. In fact, whether he has been the hapless and intellectually challenged Forrest Gump, the resourceful FedEx executive abandoned on an island, the talented lieutenant who saves Pvt. Ryan after the D-day landings, or any number of other characters, it's clear he doesn't look like Brad Pitt, and he never plays the physically aggressive and resourceful character such as Matt Damon's Jason Bourne, protagonist of two other films directed by Greenglass. In fact, of course, his characters have far more range and unpredictability than these slightly-unfair hero characterizations by other actors. In *Captain Phillips* he is a decent guy who will try to save his ship and his crew.

WE FIRST SEE Phillips as he is leaving Vermont and a comfortable life, being driven to work by his wife while talking of their kids and random social topics. Almost immediately we witness the other side to the story and the other "captain"—the life of those who become pirates, a group of semi-employed Somalis on the shore and always looking for their next job from the gatherers of the pirate skiff gangs. It's clear these people are poor, but they are also angry and a bit nasty. Though they are frightening and perhaps even terrifying, we realize they are not Somali terrorists after bodily harm or vengeance. What they want is money, but not the $30,000 in the ship's safe; they expect $10 million in ransom. (At the peak year, 117 ships were hijacked off the Somali coast, but concerted international effort has reduced those hijackings in the last few years to less than half; however, just recently there was a hijack-kidnapping off the Nigerian coast.)

THE FILM is the story of the confrontation between these two captains—and, to a lesser extent, between two cultures and two kinds of economies—between the American ship captain of a Maersk line container ship named Alabama and the pirate skiff captain with a crew of four. At one point they look at each other through binoculars, and when the skinny Somali with a lean and hungry look and an assault rifle enters the Alabama's cabin he tells Capt. Phillips to look him in the eyes and informs him, "Now I am the captain of this ship." Though he is bright and aggressive and the only member of his crew who speaks much English, he is clearly overmatched. Phillips knows his vast ship, the skinny Somali does not; the Somali and his crew have weapons, but they are vastly outnumbered, and when the Somali captain is alone, he is quickly overpowered, and a new tension begins.

There is vast imbalance between the two sides, which, after all, is one of the reasons for the prevalence of hijack-kidnapping and ransom. This imbalance is made visually powerful late in the film, when we see the escape boat containing Phillips and the Somali, a tub-shaped yellow raft from the Alabama, surrounded by three gigantic U.S. naval vessels and confronted overhead by a helicopter and eventually attacked by the famed Navy Seals dropped by parachute from a plane flying from a more remote ship. We are introduced to two more captains, the commander of the U.S. ship supervising the rescue, and the man who takes over the entire mission and orders rescue/assassinations: the leader of the Navy Seals. Both the Alabama and the U.S. Navy have tracking devices to locate the Somalis and their other skiffs and their mother ship. They also have sophisticated intelligence and a clear chain of command, and when they first encounter the Somalis, they easily remind them that they know their names, previous employments, and home addresses. Still, with all this power, five Somalis porting assault weapons in a rowboat with a powerful outboard motor have brought the Alabama and an international corporation to heel and been able to sue for ransom, at least temporarily.

We know, at some level, that the Alabama represents the power and wealth of global commerce, not to mention a namesake state of the United States, the richest nation on Earth. And it is pitted against a group of straggling serfs, former fishermen, who are widely known as members of a "failed state" with no central authority. The Somalis' apparent only source of income left is piracy on the high seas, an ancient crime, at which they have been spectacularly successful until the incident detailed in this film. Phillips in the film argues with the Somali captain, "Surely there is something for you better than kidnapping"; the response is telling: "Perhaps in America...perhaps in America."

WE SEE Captain Phillips in a series of fashion and character transformations, from the father-husband of Vermont driving to his assignment in civilian garb, to the captain in white seagoing outfit with military bars and official bearing, to the casually dressed commander of the little seagoing community, to the half-naked prisoner of the Somalis in the Alabama's lifeboat. Even in that last role, he is still compassionate, helping to dress the foot wound in one of his captors, remarking that the young man is probably only 16. In his final scene, as we last see him, rescued, he is nearly naked, stripped in the Navy ship's medical bay and so traumatized he is virtually unable to respond. He is safe, but his sense of himself has been altered—even though he will eventually return to the sea. The Somali leader is the only member of his crew to escape physically unharmed, though he will spend a long time in prison.

This is not our standard heroic ending, even though Americans have emerged seemingly triumphant. The ending leads us to ponder the various costs and outcomes and issues.

2. Double-edged Vision in *Zero Dark Thirty*

THIS FILM (2012, directed by Kathryn Bigelow) begins and ends in darkness, not even revealing its title until it's over and the credits are rolling. And it is both a mystery and "based on firsthand accounts of actual events." Is it the truth? "Where was it one first heard of the truth? The the" (Wallace Stevens). Truth is elusive. It's true that Osama bin Laden is dead. But it's hard to imagine a viewer who sees this film and wonders if that's true, or wonders if its cast of characters will eventually track down and kill UbL (to use his sometime screen nickname, creating another mystery) in Abbottabad, Pakistan, living modestly and unknown with others in a well-concealed three-story walled compound near some goats.

We've all read this on the news. Do we really go to the movies to learn the truth or to encounter history? I think not; we go to see, to be entertained, and to be challenged. This film does all of those. Some want it to do something else. Steve Coll in *The New York Review of Books*, wanted it to focus more on the lack of torture in the true hunt for UbL and wanted it to be both journalism and history. But those who expect to get their journalism and history from feature films are inevitably going to be disappointed or misled; I hope that's why there are still newspapers and books. (Those who have not seen the film and wish not to have their experience predigested or their surprises revealed should abandon this review here.)

JUST AS the film hides under an undisclosed and initially mysterious title, many characters and events in the film are similarly mysterious or double-edged or undisclosed. No one here and nothing, despite the drive of the plot, is simple. The central character Maya (Jessica Chastain), has no last name and only a dim past, and no clear friends or family and is herself a composite, presumably based on a number of CIA figures. But she is compelling, obsessed with the hunt for UbL, willing to fly to Pakistan, watch others tortured, glue herself to her computer screen, examine videos and photographs, and eat sporadically. As one of the team that will actually storm the bin Laden compound says, commenting on whether the mission will be successful, he is confident because of Maya's certainty. She appears in various guises, at different locations—in svelte Washington woman's suit, in fatigues, in discreet scarf, in niqab. She in increasing frustration writes with felt-tipped pen numbers on the glass wall of her Washington superior to remind him of the days elapsed without action since they have discovered UbL's hiding place. And in the end, she is right, but in the end, she is also very alone, in a vast C-5 cargo plane, going wherever she wants to; unfortunately, it's unclear where that might be. She has been shown to have no lover and had entered the CIA for mysterious reasons at the end of high school—like the character in *The Hurt Locker* (2008), she is a warrior who loves the hunt and her dangerous job in preference to other human ties.

OF COURSE, we meet many of Maya's colleagues and superiors, very few of whom have last names. Her closest male friend in the service, Dan, has returned to Washington from Pakistan and points East, to don a suit, and sit behind a desk because he has "seen too many men naked." Dan is willing to punish detainees, whom he talks to in a brand of apparent international slang. He offers cooperating victims food like orange drinks, tabbouleh, and hummus. He tells Maya she can take off her mask as she enters a torture session because the current victim will never see the light of day again. But Dan also has a Ph.D. and is fond of some pet monkeys on a base and grieves when he learns they have been killed. Like her CIA boss in Islamabad, Maya has been placed "on a list" and eventually has to leave the country. Her closest female friend Jessica is blown up by a bomb along with six CIA colleagues while texting Maya and awaiting the arrival in a remote Afghan outpost of a new contact with access to UbL. Jessica had baked him a cake—not a skill we associate with CIA operatives; we never know it until her death, but she left behind a husband and two children. Jessica had begun as a rival and become a friend and confidante. This surprising duality is also shown in Maya's attitude toward her immediate boss in Pakistan, whom she threatens with a congressional hearing to get his cooperation but supports sympathetically when he is forced to leave Pakistan because his CIA identity has become known. Either an ultimate irony or a recognition that this isn't really a religious war, the CIA leader who approves a key payoff is shown in Islamic prayer before he makes the decision.

THE MOVIE is about this near anonymous collection of American agents and how they go about locating and then eliminating UbL. It's not so much a detective story as a police procedural. It's about "tradecraft," a term highlighted in a subtitle and used both of Americans and of the enemy group surrounding UbL. The film uses puzzling code or abbreviations like UbL. Or KSM (Khalid Sheikh Mohammed, mastermind of 9/11) or the title itself, militarese for 0030 hours, when the assault on UbL began. The subtitles subdivide the film and offer information, but we don't easily understand how they fit together to offer a coherent narrative. One such subtitle is "The Saudi Group"—in another world or a less fraught world this might be a corporate investment group, or a bunch of CIA operatives focusing on Saudi Arabia. It is neither. A member of the Saudi group, Amar is the first detainee, the one we see interrogated, subjected briefly to waterboarding, to sound assault, to nakedness, to dog-collaring, to the "box." There are also "cordial" sessions with cooperating terrorists, high-tech listening to one's phone calls home to his Kuwaiti mother. We even see a Kuwaiti sheikh awarded a gaudy Lamborghini by securing the phone number that makes this eavesdropping possible. These all amount to the varied tradecraft strategies of detectives and hunted terrorists.

So as viewers we are enmeshed within the inevitable web of this investigative process and thoroughly stuck or drawn in. We can't extricate ourselves, we can't tear ourselves away. This is what any first-rate film or thriller does—though some great films require immense patience and concentration, and this isn't quite in that league. Most viewers who pay any attention to news know not just the outcome, but an immense percentage of what will happen. Still, we are inevitably shocked by the punctuation of this manhunt with retaliations or attacks from those who are hunted, though it is not really clear who is responsible for the inevitable and jarring interruptions to the narrative of interrogation and discovery: which is the film's main drive: to a series of explosions at points distant and close that are terrifying and terrorist events. A bombing on a London bus where no one we "know" dies, an explosion in an Islamabad hotel where Maya and Jessica are socializing and even, for a short while, relaxed. Perhaps this is a warning to Maya about trying to have a personal life, or even a beer. No one seems to die in this explosion. A black cat subtly and unnoticed glides across a roadway soon to be occupied by the vehicle which will blow up Jessica and six associates. As viewers, we never find out who plans these episodes or how they are connected. The closest we come, until the end, to UbL is his supposed courier Abu al Kuwaiti—a nom de guerre but sufficient identification ultimately to lead Maya and her cohort to his identity and his lair—who makes cellphone calls from a moving white SUV. We only see bin Laden himself at a distance and obliquely, when he is dead, lying on the top floor in Abbottabad, or the outline of his prominent nose and beard emerging from a body bag when Maya finally identifies his corpse at the attack base in Afghanistan.

The final sequence, despite its satisfying conclusion, is also disorienting and double-edged. The "Canaries" of American special forces arrive in stealth helicopters sporting headsets with multiple eyes that make them look like space aliens. The Abbottabad compound itself is a fairly domestic household of not very terrifying aging adult males, soon eliminated by American forces, surrounded by a somewhat sympathetic and cowering group of wives and children.

WHAT ARE we to make of this film? Americans like success stories, and it is a success story of effort and intense skill rewarded. It is not a defense of torture nor is it journalism nor is it history. It is not these things because it is not a narrative, a written account with an obvious single voice. This is, after all, the difference between feature film and the written word, which offers comments and almost by definition, is far more articulate. The only words the film gives us are the infrequent subtitles which locate it occasionally in space and time or seem to offer a structure…such as "Saudi Group" or "2003" or "The Canaries." But these are fragmented, as the hunt for Osama bin Laden is fragmented, and they are not actually a narrative. It is not "the truth." But it gets us or many of us to raise questions and to think about the events and especially the people that it pictures. It gets us to wonder how a Ph.D. who occasionally tortures detainees also loves feeding pet monkeys ice cream cones, and decides to retreat to a suit and Langley, how a woman with children who likes to bake cakes and is a sophisticated analyst can become vulnerable to a bomb by a contact she trusts, how Maya feels when she is finally victorious and alone after ten years of effort.

3. *All the Money in the World,* A Moral Fable

FOR WHAT shall it profit a man if he shall gain the whole world and lose his own soul? Many souls are being lost in the pursuit of wealth in this film (2017, directed by Ridley Scott). But very few souls seem worth saving, perhaps that of Paulo Getty's mother Gail (Michelle Williams), devoted to her son. risking the world and abandoning her divorce-gained custody of her other two children to get him back. Perhaps also worth saving is her aide and eventual co-conspirator, Fletcher Chase (Mark Wahlberg).

At the top of the pyramid of moral perfidy sits—guess who?—J. Paul Getty (in this version played by Christopher Plummer, but I foresee a resurrection at some point of the film's original version, where he was played by Kevin Spacey). Getty is the world's richest man—ever—and its first billionaire. But others aid and abet him or are juxtaposed against him in moral fervor or fiber or tenor. Getty's initial response to the kidnappers of his grandson Paulo, in a public statement to reporters, is what he will give as ransom: "Nothing." One of the most interesting foils for Getty is the Italian "don" who eventually takes charge of Getty's grandson (buys him, actually) in the kidnapping scheme after the first team of (inept) kidnappers fail, give up, and seek the easiest way out. This don, never identified by name, is—when we first see him, late in the film—advising employees in his fabrication sweatshop about how to better imitate high fashion goods—with more fashionable and better-sewn zippers. He is a minor businessman, admittedly corrupt, but thoughtful, in charge, and with a focus on making money. In other words, not so different from J. Paul Getty himself. The don quickly decides that the kidnapping negotiations have stalemated and he needs to move them forward. He chooses to hire the "doctor," who will sever Paulo's ear; and they will send it to the other side in the negotiations.

We see Getty bargaining with Arab sheikhs, in the 1930s or 40s, to give them a better deal than Standard Oil; we see him launching the world's first supertanker to accomplish his dreams of oil supremacy. We also see him in large touring cars, chauffeured, or in his English mansion with its extensive rooms. Or he is hidden behind doors, inaccessible to Gail, his distraught (former) daughter-in-law as she pleads for aid in rescuing her kidnapped son Paulo, appropriately enough named after his grandfather. The rooms of Getty's mansion are vast, and Getty seems comfortable, inaccessible, and alone. Many doors, gates, and servants prevent entry or access to the owner. In only a few scenes does he have human company other than hirelings—there is one intriguing scene on the grounds of his estate, where two attractive young women are firing shotguns at clay targets. Their relationship to Getty is unclear. His relations consist of estates, guns, furniture, lawyers, and expensive paintings.

There is always something a little out of focus or off-kilter about Getty. He has a series of apothegms about life and money, but in the end, most are undercut by his dubious behaviors. He tells his former daughter-in-law that he has no cash whatsoever to offer for the ransom (diminished from the original $17 million, and at this point about $10 million); however, in a following scene we see Getty pay $1 million in cash for an allegedly noteworthy painting of dubious provenance that he is warned not to display publicly.

OTHERS JUDGED in the film are the original kidnappers, venal, amoral, but not particularly violent or without humane characteristics. The one guarding Paulo, Cinquanta (apparently his nickname, "50"), frequently lets his mask drop so that Paulo could identify him. Later, at the climax, when Paulo is freed, Cinquanta appears suddenly in an Italian village street and stuns one of Paulo's pursuers with a deft blow. The "doctor" is efficient, knowledgeable, undoubtedly compensated (but not according to medical standards of insurance companies) and severs Paulo's ear, which we witness in painful detail; the young man gets no anesthetic, and neither do we. Meanwhile, families of Italians associated with the kidnappers diligently do laundry, bustle about rooms, do the dishes, and don't seem particularly bothered by the essential human transaction at the center. The don has about ten women in a room diligently counting the ransom without any particular emotion.

Paulo's father is perhaps the saddest case of all: as he ages in the film, he goes from assistant to his father to drug-addict to Moroccan deadbeat. He appears spectrally at the kidnap negotiations—though he is clearly still on drugs—apparently to assume custody of the other children in exchange for the ransom money.

Fletcher Chase appears to occupy the shifting moral middle ground. He's far more sophisticated and knowledgeable about the details of kidnapping and ransom than his employer, and he is skilled at what he does. He informs Gail he doesn't carry a gun because it's not helpful in these situations and only gets in the way. Yet on the Getty estate, next to the two female clay pigeon shooters, when he is handed a shotgun he casually lowers it and hits two targets simultaneously. He knows what he is doing. Yet he is too easily convinced that his employer is being scammed by a "joke" perhaps launched by the grandson and daughter-in-law and tells Getty to back off. Actually, only a casual remark and a rumor were enough to launch this withdrawal. As he discovers, essentially, his employer's indifference and inhumanity, he switches sides and helps Gail negotiate and get the final money and is present at the exchange of kid for ransom, which doesn't go as expected. Paulo eventually survives his captors' attempted recapture/murder of him and is returned to his mother. In a following scene, we see Getty apparently entirely alone in his mansion suffering a fatal stroke or heart attack. Despite his attempt to disinherit his former daughter-in-law and sever her children from her custody, Getty had made her executor of the trust and the estate presumably because he recognized she is level-headed and rational, and the only possible family member responsible enough and not addicted to drugs to take charge, so she takes over.

Paulo himself is first seen as a longhaired teenager (he was 16 when he was kidnapped) ambling the late night Roman streets, apparently looking for drugs or prostitutes—but aimlessly and not very intently. The opening prostitutes are suggestive symbols of all the figures in the film for whom money is an evasion or sale of fundamental human commodities. When a passerby warns the young man to be careful, he assures that person that he is savvy and can take care of himself—apparently because he knows some Italian. Nevertheless, in the very next moments, he is hustled into the kidnap van thinking it's a solicitation from a prostitute. He is also the recipient when he is young of an archeological artifact from his grandfather—attended with tales of its provenance and great value. After his mother remembers the gift, in the middle of negotiations, and searches frantically to find it in her apartment, Sotheby's experts inform her it is worth but a few dollars. Not that all of this is entirely convincing; supposedly Gail is broke, and two months behind in rent, but she is always seen smartly dressed and lives in large, well-furnished apartments and can travel to England quite quickly. Presumably, the child support is very generous, but not much is made of this factor.

AT THE center of this film are wealth and its assumptions and consequences, hardly viewed favorably. The current President of the U.S. is reputedly a billionaire. The film claims Getty was the first billionaire, but despite the American focus on amassing wealth, there are very few artistic (as opposed to biographical) studies of those who actually accumulate it. In films, perhaps the iconic study is Charles Foster Kane of *Citizen Kane*, with its analytic echoes of William Randolph Hearst. Like Getty, Kane dies alone, apparently longing for his childhood security (Rosebud)—a bit corny. The moral seems to be that wealth is isolating and destructive. Perhaps a more sympathetic portrait of a famous, but reclusive plutocrat of the same era is that of Howard Hughes in *The Aviator*: a tormented and near-psychotic figure who is also somehow capable of inventive engineering, daredevil flying, canny business decisions, and attracting admiring women. Yet there *have* been "good" billionaires in American life, to a greater and lesser degree, depending on one's perspective: Warren Buffett, Michael Bloomberg, Andrew Carnegie (often unsung lately, but responsible initially for most of the public libraries in the U.S.). Even William Randolph Hearst—in real life, as opposed to his movie alter ego Kane—was a relatively happy man, though he had bad taste in recreating castles. In the film Getty lives in a castle in England and is trying to build one in Malibu. Getty was a notorious penny-pincher, to the point of comedy, incivility, and—as emphasized in this film—

ultimately inhumanity. He installed a pay phone in his house so guests, visitors, and workmen could not freeload long distance calls. While trying to negotiate the ransom and deal with her family in Rome, Gail is forced to use it, but one of Getty's servants loans her the many coins necessary. Getty doesn't want to pay the 17-million-dollar ransom originally demanded; in fact, he is initially willing to pay nothing, arguing at the time that his refusal to pay protects his other 14 grandchildren from kidnapping and, actually (though not in the film), that his stance is a principled response to terrorism, violence, and the overall breakdown of order, though it is clearly just cheapness. As the negotiations advance, the ransom is lowered to $10, then $7, then $5 million. Getty eventually gives in, limiting his contribution to what his attorneys assert would be tax deductible; on top, he gives part of it as a loan to his son, so he can deduct interest.

Though the film shows the billionaire dying just after his grandson is rescued, Getty actually waited a full four years to die. Like any art form, the film takes liberties with fact—with history—to heighten the dramatic tension. Though it portrays Paulo's father as completely drug-addicted and worthless, he was the first in the family to ask his father for the ransom. At the end, we have the sense that Paulo is rescued, and that his mother, poetically justified, takes guardianship of the estate. But Paulo never really emerged from the trauma of the kidnapping, returned to drug addiction, became paralyzed through a drug/alcohol overdose, and died at 54.

The epilogue shows us a version of the Malibu estate, where Getty's wealth apparently went after his death—it was turned into a premiere art gallery. But some of its holdings are redolent of the deal Getty makes in the film, for a painting of dubious vintage and supposedly bought on the cheap.

4. The Past Revisited and Restored: *Woman in Gold*

THE 2015 film *Woman in Gold* (directed by Simon Curtis) is based on a true story and retells it with some detail, intelligence, and passion. At the center of the story is an actual portrait by an Austrian painter of the early twentieth century, Gustav Klimt, of a friend and patron, Adele Bloch-Bauer, surrounded by ornamentation in shimmering gold.

When the story begins, the painting remains in a museum in Vienna, but the niece of Adele, Maria Altman (played by Helen Mirren) claims the painting is due her as an inheritance. The film retraces Maria's legal efforts to retrieve the painting from the Austrian museum and government, and the pain and memories these efforts cause her.

Adele Bloch-Bauer I shows a woman in a decorative design of gold with many other iconographic symbols, to the point where the decoration seems to overwhelm the mysterious woman and expand into the painting's background, while transforming her into a goddess or an object of worship. (It's "Adele Bloch-Bauer **I**" because Klimt named it that and did a second portrait of her in a different, less arresting style. It's called "Woman in Gold" by the Belvedere art museum, the Vienna museum where it is kept, making it more universal but perhaps also obscuring its roots.) The painting is now world famous and, as the film has it, a refrigerator magnet icon that somehow symbolizes the Secession art movement, a Byzantine past, Klimt, and Austria itself. Adele and her husband, from a tight-knit, successful Viennese Jewish family, are friends and patrons of Klimt, himself somewhat of a Bohemian figure, but his artistry and life are soon eclipsed in the film by the sufferings of the Bloch-Bauers and Vienna's Jews when the Nazis don't so much invade as assume power.

The painting, along with others, was acquired by the government of Austria after the Anschluss, or union, of Austria and Germany in 1938. The joining of Austria and Germany had an 80% approval rating in Austria when it was initially suggested by Hitler. This may have been a celebratory time in Vienna, but it inaugurated a painful time for Vienna's Jews, and this corner of the Holocaust is one of the film's centers. In flashbacks and cross-cuttings to that era we see Maria and her family observing Jews forced to wash sidewalks and be publicly humiliated. Swastika-draped officials take over her family's apartment, placing the family in effect under house arrest, and confiscate their paintings and jewels because of an alleged tax evasion by Maria's father.

PAINFUL AS these scenes are, they are essentially fleeting, as most of the film is set in the recent present with Maria and her lawyer Randol Schoenberg's struggle to assert her ownership of the painting (along with other Klimts previously owned by her uncle). The lawyer (played by Ryan Reynolds), also Jewish and with his own claim to Austrian nobility through his famous relative the composer Anton Schoenberg, is reluctant at first to take on the case and wonders—in the California of the 1990s (Maria lives in California)—why Maria seems so obsessed with events of "50 years ago." But he soon discovers, via Google, that the Klimt painting may be worth $130 million dollars. The key story and the film's emotional center is in the growing understanding and respect between Maria and Randol. She sees he is dogged and imaginative in his pursuit of her (and her family's) rights, and he is so moved when he goes to Vienna and visits the tomblike Holocaust memorial that he retreats to a men's room to vomit. The closeness that grows between them is not only the result of his tragic recognition of the Holocaust's suffering but of their shared sense during the legal battle that their Austrian opponents are disingenuous and self-serving—or that is certainly the black-white moral view of the film. The Austrian art director of the Belvedere is not interested in any accommodation (e.g., recognition of Altman's rights to the painting in exchange for an extended loan to the Belvedere), until he loses the case.

Maria sticks by her young, somewhat inexperienced, lawyer with shallow pockets even when she is offered the financial aid and vast legal services of the Estee Lauder fortune, whose heir later founded a museum on New York's 5th Avenue to permanently display the Klimt. Lauder, at a luncheon, offers his highly trained, well-respected lawyer, whom he suggests she should prefer to a schoolboy. Maria says she'll go with her boy. Maria's and Randol's growing trust and affection is at the film's center. Helen Mirren's Maria is distinguished by girlishly rearranging her hair several times throughout the film and by her arch and often comic responses; she has a sense of humor that often borders on the sarcastic. But her character is also modest, really expecting little more initially than a chance to replace her aging dishwasher. She is confident, but clearly haunted by memories of her Viennese past and the painful events that led to her lifelong exile.

The film is stuck with a plot dilemma. For all the suspense and inherent drama of a legal case that pits a lone individual against history and the vast resources of a sovereign government, restoring the paintings cannot bring back the past, cannot restore the dead aunt (Adele, with a history of medical problems, died young, years before the Anschluss) or the suffering parents left behind in Vienna, or the thousands of Jews sent to their deaths in a variety of camps and memorialized in the Holocaust monument in Vienna. This is, alas, the ultimate truth of all such legal cases. However, the two principals do not simply take the money and run. Maria sells the Klimts to a museum in New York where they can regularly be seen by the public, and donates much of her gain to charity; Randol also designates a significant portion of his fees to charitable purposes.

Still missing from this account is some sense of what the artwork itself represents and the lively world of fin-de-siècle Vienna, its Jews (among whom numbered Sigmund Freud), and the bohemian art milieu of Gustav Klimt, many of whose paintings featured nudes, and who for years dressed in a unisex fashion along with his lover, as a comment on what they considered impractical public standards of dress. Also not shown or mentioned are Klimt's beautiful paintings of parks and castles and trees, far different from those of his gold decorative period and rivaling those of the Post-Impressionists for color and intensity and imagination. But no film can do everything.

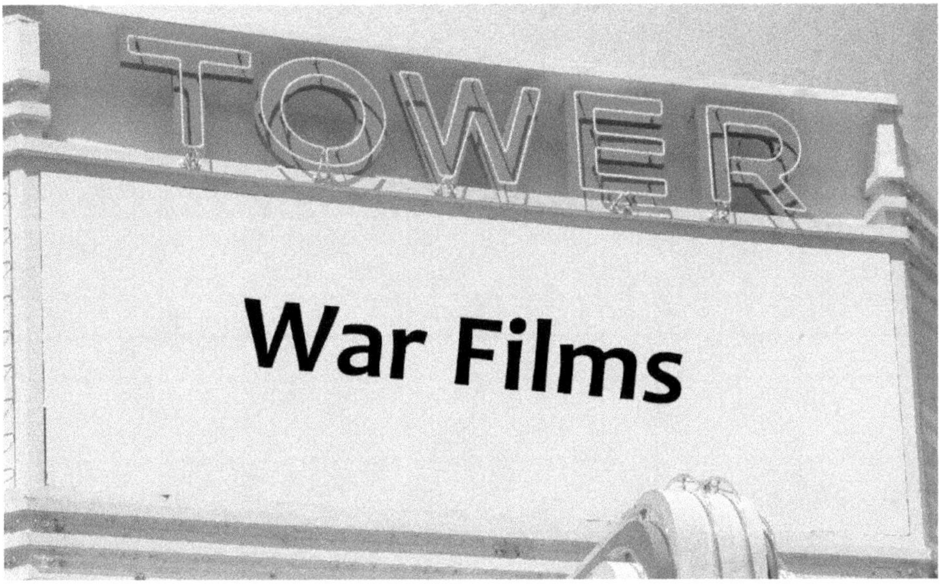
TOWER
War Films

5. Two War Films: Can Art Rescue Us from World War II?
The Book Thief
and
The Monuments Men

THE OSCARS have just been awarded, and I'm going to write about two films that those Oscars largely ignored, for different reasons: *The Book Thief*, because it got nominated in only one category and seemed a minor film in comparison with the others; and *The Monuments Men*, because it opened too late to be considered for this year's Oscars. Both are films about World War II and, for me at least, raise interesting questions about that key twentieth century event, which, for most of us in 2014, some 70 years after its ending, is just history, the past, but each succeeding year is still good for a film or two.

The war is attractive for a variety of reasons, I guess, a kind of somber gift that keeps on giving: its geographical reach was so vast and its social penetration so varied and so deep, that there's always a new story to be told, or one that was somehow missed. And also, as viewers, we think we know the moral: the good guys, the U.S. and the Allies (including, of course, the Russians, who suffered greater losses than any other country, though that comparative factor is often ignored or elided in the American imagination), won in the end, and they were fighting a figure, Hitler, almost universally associated with evil. But do we, can we, really know? Do we actually understand that war or its significance? As so often, I have to warn you that, though I recommend seeing both films, I'm going to disclose so much information in the following paragraphs that you might want to skip them until you've seen the movies themselves.

THE BOOK THIEF got a lot of play in advance, in previews, in reviews. And it is a film that touches the heart and brought me to tears at the end, kind of by surprise. At the finale the audience applauded, an experience I don't encounter very often in movie-going. The outlines of the story are simple—a young girl in Nazi Germany during World War II, displaced and vulnerable, who finds a kind of human compensation for loss and fear in stealing and reading books. Liesl (Sophie Nélisse) is half an orphan who has been shipped to this German town and adopted after her mother is forced to abandon her (we are never sure why). She begins her first day at the local school by being forced to write her name on the blackboard—but all she can produce are 3 X's—for she is illiterate. But her kindly adoptive father Hans (Geoffrey Rush) reads with her and constructs a giant dictionary on the walls of the basement to improve her vocabulary; then Max, the wandering Jew her adoptive parents have hidden in the basement, encourages her to describe the outside world in new metaphors and gives her a journal as a present to hold those descriptions.

I'M PROBABLY not the only viewer reminded by this film of *The Reader* (2008), an Academy Award winner that also dealt with the Nazi period and focused, sympathetically, on another illiterate figure, played by Kate Winslet (Hanna Schmitz). We first see Hanna in the early 1930s in Germany in a sexual relationship with a much younger man who reads to her and through whom the whole experience of the film is eventually seen. Hanna confronts us with the moral quandary of a lifelong illiterate who becomes a concentration camp guard and then is placed on trial with others for their crimes in the camp; Hanna so much wants to hide her illiteracy that she takes responsibility for acts that were shared. We are left, as is the protagonist, with the question of how to fully and fairly judge her.

The Book Thief is less stark, less morally startling than that earlier film, and it wins us over because Liesl, the young reader who begins in illiteracy is so innocent, so charming, and so kind. The film is also marked by an unusual narrator, Death himself: At some level Germany 1938-45 (the primary span of the film's time) is an all-encompassing world of death, and virtually everyone is suffering or will suffer some kind of loss—but there is essentially much normal life still going on, walks to school, childhood flirtations, schoolyard bullies, secrets, and mysteries. And Death is, apparently, all-knowing and inclusive, for he takes us up not only to the end of the war but to Liesl's death, in the twenty-first century, when she has become a successful writer and led a happy life in, apparently, Manhattan. Death reminds us we will all meet him. Somehow I doubt that this is the most sophisticated or morally profound observation on World War II, true and regrettable though it may be.

Yet the Germany we experience in the film, despite patriotic songs in school, basement searches by SS officers, ubiquitous giant red flags with swastikas, and a refreshingly dramatic mass book-burning early in the film, is treated very generously. The SS officer we see searching basements (and worry he may find Max hiding in Liesl's family's basement) is not seeking hidden Jews, but only looking for adequate underground storage to serve as air-raid shelters during nighttime bombings. The songs sung at school assert Germany's ascendance and its dislike of aliens, Jews, non-Germans, and so forth—but there is no accompanying bitterness or cruelty to heighten these songs. The only figure of clear malevolence in the film is the schoolyard bully, an ardent Nazi, Franz, whom Liesl easily beats up in a fight.

IN FACT, nearly all the characters in *The Book Thief* turn out to be endearing—Liesl's adoptive mother Rosa, who at first seems harsh, bitter, and uncaring, in contrast to the kindly and forgiving stepfather, comes to school in a harsh mood and calls out Liesl, but we learn she has used the rough exterior superficially associated with her reputation to hide her relief that their hidden tenant, Max the Jew, hasn't died from a wintery fever, but has recovered. The burgomaster, who presides at the book-burning and lives in a stately mansion at the edge of town, has a wife who befriends Liesl and invites her to the well-stocked mansion library to read books—some of which Liesl eventually steals (actually borrows: despite the title, we only see her borrowing and returning two or three books).

Given the deathly narrator and the war setting, there are certainly direct reminders that this was far from a pleasant, peaceful, or humane existence—there is one scene of brown-shirts breaking windows and beating merchants during Kristallnacht in Stuttgart, another of Jews with yellow stars marched through the streets of Liesl's town by unsympathetic German officers, and then there is the unannounced air raid that results in Death's claim on Liesl's adoptive parents, her young boyfriend Rudy and his family, and many others. Still Max and Liesl survive the war, as of course did most others. And we realize she grew because of the kindnesses of many friends and the power of words and literature.

That's consoling, but the continued voice-overs by Death seem artificial, contrived, unnecessary. And somehow the treatment of the German village is oddly sanitized.

THE MONUMENTS MEN, based on actual experiences of a small unit of American soldiers, is, like *The Book Thief*, devoted to the idea that art is the key element to survive the war. But in this latter case, men fight for it, and in a series of comments mostly as narratorial voiceovers, attempt to justify their pursuit. Despite its ground-hold in actual military and historical realities (or perhaps because of it), and despite an all-star cast with talented character actors and a few memorable moments, *Monuments Men* is oddly disappointing, like a cartoon or a sketch or a pastiche of a World War II film. After every sequence there is something lacking, something missing, or there has been a clear compromise or simplification or appeal to sentimentality.

The most obvious instance of this kind of subtle but repeated failure is the background music, which becomes annoying and obtrusive. It's constantly changing, constantly encouraging viewers in how to read scenes, especially when the men rediscover, or recover, supposedly great works of art, but neither the actors nor the scenes nor the music nor the art works themselves are that impressive.

The crusade to recover stolen works of art from the retreating Nazi troops in the last year of the war is oddly disappointing and unconvincing. Perhaps it is the lack of marquee art works at the center. Undoubtedly the most famous art work threatened is Da Vinci's "The Last Supper," painted on a wall in Milan, in a building that collapses due to bombardment. We see this painting, in the film's chaotic mosaic structure, but it's never woven into the plot, nor does the American Monuments Men unit save that art work. Instead the two key works they save are a Madonna and Son by Michelangelo (preeminent, allegedly, because it's his only sculpture outside Italy) and the Ghent altarpiece. Along the way in the background are a Vermeer and a minor Rembrandt, but they seem only footnotes; we also see the charred frame that once held a Picasso. When the soldiers of the unit finally locate and uncover the hidden Michelangelo piece, there is a moment and some music, but nothing like the reverse tracking shot showing surprise and astonishment that Jean Renoir employed in a truly great war film, *The Grand Illusion* (1937).

So THE arguments that the film seems to want to make—that these great art works are our heritage, are threatened with extinction, and are worth military effort to save—just aren't very convincing or compelling. But it keeps making these arguments in a number of forms and scenes, nonetheless. That something other than human lives and dignity should be saved from the morass of such a conflagration is perhaps ennobling, that art itself may hold the key to human persistence and transcendence is satisfying, but each time the film states some version of this, it is underwhelming. *Saving Private Ryan* (1998) kept offering a number of explanations for what to its platoon appeared to me a misguided mission, to save one near-anonymous soldier in the aftermath of D-day, and these were arguments ultimately about the value of the war itself; yet they had some resonance and depth and kept varying—because it is not easy to offer such vindications.

Frank Stokes (George Clooney) persuades President Roosevelt to create the Monuments Men corps because victory in the war would be hollow if all human art were lost. But as the film develops it appears to be an effort to prevent the Germans from stealing major European art works for a Hitler Museum in his hometown of Linz, Austria. However, if the allies win the war, as they are clearly going to do when Stokes is initially martialing his arguments and later his men, such a museum would never come to pass. He assures the President and asks his men to take care that no life be lost in the quest to rescue the art, yet two of his men die.

The Michelangelo pieta and the Ghent altarpiece that are sought are public art of the type belonging to public institutions, yet James Granger (Matt Damon) is intent on saving a group of artworks in Paris that the

Germans have stolen from private collectors—in the event all French Jews—and altruistically not capturing them for the Metropolitan Museum of Art, of which he will eventually become curator, but to return them to their owners. Sadly, these owners are likely to have perished in the Holocaust. In one of the film's sequences I *do* find powerful, Granger reads the address inscribed on the side of a painting and returns it to the abandoned apartment in Paris where it had once resided and hangs it on the wall in the faded space it once shadowed, because, as he says, he feels that's where it should be.

In another plot strand of the film, the effort of the American Monuments Men is to track down key art stolen by the Germans to prevent the Russians (American allies) from finding it and stealing it to reside in some museum in the Soviet Union. To some extent, this absurd contest, which the Americans in the film win, merely reminds us that victorious war (or power or state wealth) in Europe has historically yielded art troves for great powers—hence the great collection of Breughels in the museum in Vienna, or the wealth of art in the Prado or....

The wider question of who really owns the art or where it should be is not actually addressed, except to say where it used to be before the war. Near film's and war's end, now-President Truman asks now-Major Stokes the same question about whether the recovery of the art was worth the military effort, and a voiceover effects a transition to 1977, when a grandfatherly and aging Stokes visits the Ghent altarpiece with his grandson and answers, "Yes it was." This is rhetorically powerful and reassuring, perhaps an echo of the fictional Pvt. Ryan's question at the end of his film, whether the deaths of his comrades in saving his life was worth it. Unfortunately, the Ghent altarpiece is no more aesthetically powerful nor moving, and this echo of the ending of *Saving Private Ryan*, where an aging Ryan with wife and daughters visits the Normandy graves of the men who saved him, isn't very convincing. It simply seems another place where *Monuments Men* has reached an aesthetic and moral dead end and run out of creativity and gas. And, sadly, the film elides or collapses key moral questions of who owns art, or whether the victors are entitled to some of the spoils, whether they are Germans or Americans or Russians. No one bothers to ask whether the "Elgin Marbles," which used to adorn the Parthenon in Athens and now remain in a beautiful, elegant room in the British Museum, should be returned to the Greeks.

The film runs out of such gas often, particularly in dialogue. One of the Monuments Men is killed, and Stokes receives word by phone and comments, "It's a hell of a thing." He tells a colleague, who echoes, "It's a hell of a thing." Without consulting the book on which this is based, I suspect this is what someone remembers saying, but it's hardly imaginative, memorable, moving, or worth preserving. The best we could say is, if it's accurate, or "true," it acknowledges the inarticulate fumbling of human beings when they confront suffering, tragedy, or loss.

The film's confusion is repeatedly seen in its mixed, episodic, and accidental structure, apparently trying to cull together as many events from the actual history of this art corps as might interest a viewer. So we get one sequence where Stokes shows Roosevelt and others a giant map of Europe with the advances of the allies portrayed—presumably more for the contemporary audience and its perhaps questionable geography than, one would hope, for four or five men running the most serious war in modern history. In a series of other sequences, we see the Monuments Men land after D-day; we see Granger flown to Paris by a member of the Resistance who retrieves a propeller plane from a barn (he probably did, but so what? it's a sequence with much promise, but it doesn't lead in any coherent direction); we see titled sequences identifying allied "progress" like "Remagen" or "The Battle of the Bulge." But the Bulge battle is an odd sequence, with nothing like the sense of threat, surprise, loneliness, and eeriness, for example, of the parallel battle in the TV mini-series *Band of Brothers* (2001)....

The odd thing is that in *Monuments Men* there is no battle whatsoever, just a group of men rambling between large tents across a field. For me the film's most memorable scene shows architect Richard Campbell (Bill Murray) getting a record from his Chicago family singing "Have Yourself a Very Merry Christmas" ; he is allowed to hear it over the camp radio while taking a camp shower, through the graces of Preston Savitz (Bob Balaban), his rival and angry friend, who arranges to have it played. This is the only music in the film that has some effect and "works"; it grows out of the situation, is actually played by the characters, as opposed to added later, as background; however, it's still a distant echo of the same song played in *The Godfather* (1972).

There are perhaps expected set pieces, where the unit's translator, the only Jewish soldier, finally gets to see the Rembrandt self-portrait he was forbidden while growing up in a racist Germany; or where a captured German officer, questioned by Major Stokes, refuses to provide any information and assumes he will be repatriated without punishment even though he ran a concentration camp and then alleges that since Stokes isn't Jewish the officer's extermination campaign did him a favor, but is then instead threatened with hanging.

The Monuments Men do recover a great deal of art, some 1,400 pieces, and also find a mound of gold bars hidden in a mine, as well as a barrel of gold teeth (extracted in the camps from exterminated human beings). But in a way, these are all side shows, because the film is so lost in purpose.

PERHAPS THE conclusion to draw from both *The Book Thief* and *The Monuments Men* is that art might provide some solace from such a tragic and terrible war, but it's still stumbling to do so—even after 70 years.

6. War & Art Part I:
Dunkirk

IN MY unrelenting search for something worthwhile to feast my eyes on in late afternoon or early evening and take me from the Trump-drenched world to other worlds worth contemplating, while munching on the obligatory bag of unbuttered popcorn, I recently saw two films, *Dunkirk* and *Maudie*. The titles, as so frequently, tell you very little—the names of places or people or events—and they promise very little, unless you happen to know about these things in advance. They don't really tell you about content or feeling or approach. You're supposed to learn these on your own, through general cultural knowledge, or the deluge of previews in previous visits to movie houses. And I probably see more previews than the average moviegoer, trying to get my movie fix at least twice a week, arriving early to locate a suitable seat and to see previews.

So here are two more movies that are inarticulate—in title at least—about uttering their intentions or tone: you have to know, to know. So far this 52 weeks, the most opaque title in this regard was *Manchester by the Sea*, which told us nothing about the suffering and loss and trauma at the film's center.

WILL THIS guy ever get to talking about the films themselves? Yes. They are actually two very opposite and worthwhile films in their own way. *Dunkirk*, which, judging by its prevalence in most of the theaters where I live, and its deluge of previews in the 3-5 months before, is a film most of you will see and be familiar with, or so I assume. It's a film about World War II, the war that keeps on giving. In the three and a half years it existed, from an American perspective, it absorbed the attention, treasure, and in some cases, lives of Americans (though many more Americans died in the Civil War, 620,000 v. the 408,000 dead in World War II; yet of course far fewer films have emerged from our civil war). This tide of movies and art about the War, fascinating in its absorption, shows no sign of ceasing, though movie makers have looked into so many of its little-known side stories, such as the *The Monuments Men* sent to preserve works of art, or *Woman in Gold,* about a stolen work of art, to name only two of recent vintage. And now we have the current one with its focus on Dunkirk, technically and actually a battle that didn't absorb us (i.e., Americans), as it was fought by the British and French and Germans in May and June 1940 before the U.S. entered the war.

But we still know of it, know enough to think of Dunkirk, or *Dunkerque* (French, possibly with a Belgian language influence), as a historical moment tied to a place, which most of us can't find readily on the map: it's at the upper right-hand, east, corner of France's Atlantic coast, on the Belgian border and abutting the English Channel. From the map, Dunkirk seems the closest location on the European mainland to England—it's about 40 miles away—but actually Calais is a bit closer to the English coast. Compare this to the distance from the British coast to the Normandy beaches, site of the counterattack on D-Day, almost four years later to the day—about 100 miles. The way back is much harder! The Germans blitzed through France in a month; the Allies, despite far superior strength and a near foregone conclusion, fought their path across the Channel to the heart of Germany and into Berlin in about a year.

DUNKIRK WAS, in effect, the conclusion of the early British-French war with Nazi Germany and an abrupt and surprising endpoint in what turned out to be the early stages of a war that was declared (by the Allies) in September 1939; yet little physical fighting took place until May 1940. Once the Germans attacked, on 10 May, it took them essentially three weeks to sweep across Northern France and reach the coast, almost cutting off the remaining Allied troops from withdrawal. The actual evacuation of Dunkirk is usually dated May 26-June 4, 1940, less than two weeks. About 340,000 troops of the British Expeditionary Force were evacuated in the 9 days of the process, some from the "harbor," some directly from the beaches. This still left about 70,000 British troops who had been left behind or died in France. Nevertheless, the evacuation is considered one of the war's key opening events and offered a glimmer of hope to those fighting Hitler; it concluded, as the film does, with Churchill's iconic speech that "We shall fight them on the beaches...we shall never surrender."

Most of this previous two paragraphs of history is assumed, implied, or elided by the film, which like most war films, is required to actually tell a story with characters. War is a vast, brutal enterprise that at some level—or some point—is a battle of statistics, in which humans, as Hemingway once suggested, are like ants being burned on a log by an indifferent god, numerous and somehow unimportant. But we respond to war because of the anecdotes, the personal stories, whether it is those of *Saving Private Ryan* or those of *Dunkirk*. The current movie begins dramatically with a British soldier fleeing bullets through the streets of an apparently deserted French town, mostly full of ruins, barriers, or bulwarks. Drifting through the air are a multitude of mysterious flyers notifying the recipients that they are surrounded by German forces. We never see the source of these bullets or whence the flyers issued; when they stop for a while, they seem to resume around the next barricade or corner, though the laws of physics and logic suggest that they do not come from the same source. Eventually we see the soldier make it to the beach at Dunkirk, where slow, endless lines of men stand about in single file, apparently waiting to make it into boats. They also line up for the "mole," one of the remaining piers along which embarkation is still possible.

ANOTHER ASPECT of war that the film "gets right" is its relentless unpredictability and frustration. In fact, for the two central characters (two Allied troops), the escape from Dunkirk is a representative series of failures and near-mortal frustrations. They try to embark on a departing ship by running a wounded soldier on a stretcher past an endless line of waiting embarkees but are rejected at the ship's plank because they are not medical personnel. Though they hide on the pier and jump on another ship, they are nearly drowned when it is attacked, capsizes, and floods. They flounder in the oily water and appear to catch fire. One of the two, returned to the beach, takes shelter inside a transport stranded by low tide and soon filling with other refugees; as the tide rises, tiny holes appear in the bow, increasingly obvious as bullet holes; the inhabitants cower from the unseen source and try to plug the holes, as the rising tide comes through them into the boat.

So, at the film's center are these linked stories of the two soldiers—one British, one anonymous and temporarily mute (but actually French; he has tried to disguise his identity because initially the only combatants being rescued are British)—who like most of the historical British soldiers lining the beach, escape. By film's end they are riding on a British train taking them from Dover, drinking beer, and casually reading news of the miraculous success of the evacuation, listening to Churchill's heroic speech. We know from history that the film's narrative arc is moving toward this end, though, as a retreat and an evacuation, it is hardly a clear triumph, except that so many stranded combatants are unexpectedly saved.

THERE ARE three other parallel narrative arcs in the films: the story of a few British pilots, who protect troops and ships, while gradually being shot down; the story of a single British civilian sloop relentlessly proceeding to Dunkirk to pick up survivors; and the decisions of the commanding British officer, played by Kenneth Branagh, to get the troops "home" (i.e., Britain, which he reminds them is so close), himself staying too long almost stranded on the French shore. At moments of key suspense, the background noise/music swells in an increasing tempo of mechanical sounding tones that I found increasingly artificial and annoying: I can tell when there's suspense, especially one created by a series of cuts and forward motion lasting seemingly forever.

Though this is only a sliver of the vast and branching tree that was the second World War, it is still, like every war film, from a limited and narrowed perspective: in this case, that of the retreating forces. We know, throughout the film, that these bullets and bombs and shells come from the Nazis, but we never actually see one, until the sole British pilot from the subplot exhausts his fuel, lands safely on the Dunkirk sands, sets fire to his plane, and is arrested nonviolently by German soldiers. The French, who held off some of the German forces while the British evacuated (and were themselves then partially evacuated to Britain) are seen only in one early shot and represented in the second, seemingly taciturn, of the two fleeing soldiers.

THERE ARE some great directorial and cinematic decisions in this film, but it is hard for me to say how oddly they are insufficient, unsatisfying. Perhaps it is that the three central stories, like so many in war, are radically disconnected and, in the end, unsurprisingly lead to a "happy" ending. The two escaping soldiers make it to Britain, the rescue ship rescues many and brings them back, the British pilot survives dogfights and protects evacuees and finds a way to survive. Somehow, I had expected more from Christopher Nolan, the famed director who first came to attention with *Memento* (2000, Nolan's second film), about a man tattooing information about the present on his body and living backward in time. Eventually we learn he is like the mythical Alzheimer sufferer who experiences joy in hiding and recovering his own Easter eggs, because he cannot remember anything from one moment to the next. Nolan was also the directorial force behind *The Dark Knight* trilogy, *The Prestige*, and *Interstellar*.

It's probably unfair to offer a critique of a single war film when so few have been truly remarkable. It's just not that easy to make a serious and meaningful film about anything so vast and complex and painful and contradictory as war. This is the second film about Dunkirk; the first, also British, came out in 1958, with significantly different subplots. Probably the most recent war film worth remembering is *Saving Private Ryan*, which, for the half-hour of its transcription of the D-day landings at the opening, is remarkable for its sheer visual terror and gore and for its power to dissuade young teens from being enthusiastic about warfare. Sadly, *Saving Private Ryan* meanders toward its predictable heroic end (Ryan saved, all his altruistic defenders/protectors killed: a fairly thin reed on which to balance the purpose for all the American actions in the Second World War). But in its D-day depiction, it was far superior to an earlier incarnation, *The Longest Day*, based on the anecdotal and exhaustive nonfiction reportage of Cornelius Ryan. For the earlier film was merely an entertaining and amusing collection of individual stories of survival and disaster, with little to connect them: a dilemma imposed by the very nature of a day of warfare itself—it struggled with the tension between history and narrative. In that film, the landings themselves were oddly bloodless and seem, now by contrast, almost lifeless: when anyone died that day in that film, they had been shot, and just fell over hitting the sand as if they were going to sleep early: unlike *Saving Private Ryan*, they didn't lose an arm and search for it, or call out in agony for their mothers, or were burned alive screaming in pain. Sadly, in Nolan's *D5nkirk*, soldiers are again just falling over to denote death, though the terror and fear of wounding and bombing seem real and ever-present.

Dunkirk* is what used to be called a blockbuster of a film: major director and major star (Kenneth Branagh, though he actually has a minor role), months-long lead-up in previews in theaters and on television, playing in virtually every multiplex simultaneously on opening day.

We have also seen its closing speech again in the recent Churchill film, *The Darkest Hour;* but in the latter film we see the speech from the perspective of political management, personal confrontation, and rhetoric.

See review 19, "War and Art Part II: Maudie," for the completion of this   essay.

7. The Post:
The War Goes On

PERHAPS IT'S just my imagination or prejudices, but it seems to me an inordinate number of recent feature films—supposedly a form of film fiction, and hopefully art forms in themselves—are either infinite sequels of mildly successful previous films, or retellings of actual events (history or news in some sense). What's missing, more frequently than before, are fiction films that create characters that probe deeply into what's behind history or human character or behavior. I suppose to some extent, this is a false dichotomy, and there have been very good films made from actual historical events: I could mention, e.g., *Patton*. But when I go through my deep mental catalog of great intriguing films, they are nearly all fiction films, even if their origins are murky or dubious or quasi-historical: *The Rules of the Game, Shoot the Piano Player, Citizen Kane, The Godfather, McCabe and Mrs. Miller*. This is a brief list, but for me it seems representative.

Having launched this mild resistance to the glut of films about historical events or figures, I willingly admit that the film of that genre under consideration here—*The Post*—is a film of serious artistic merit, but to me it also seems to lack some far deeper dimension, because, whatever it is, it is essentially a retelling of actual and momentous historical events. So, for example, are *Dunkirk, The Darkest Hour*, and *I Tonya*, though the last is not about *momentous* historical events; intriguingly the first two overlap in their focus on the same quintessential and brief historical period, the spring of 1940.

THE POST, like so many films, is misleadingly and ambiguously titled, since it is hardly about the entire or even the summary history or experience of *The Washington Post*. It doesn't even begin with the historic *Post* but with warfare in the jungles of Vietnam and the experience of Daniel Ellsberg and Secretary of Defense Robert McNamara. The real focus is on the publication of the Pentagon Papers, supposedly revealing all the government secrets and judgments and misjudgments about the war from Truman to Eisenhower to Kennedy to Johnson, and the roles of Katharine Graham, publisher of the *Post*, and Ben Bradlee, its editor—and of Ellsberg—in their publication.

SINCE IT is a newspaper story, or a story about how the personnel at a newspaper go about finding and vetting information, there is a lot of moving of actors in and about crowded city rooms, with desks and doors and obstruction. So, the early "action" in Vietnam is replaced by movement in offices, in homes, and across city streets (mainly young men running across the street, defying traffic) to the *New York Times* building in New York (the *Times* had been the first to work intensely on the story of the Pentagon Papers and to begin publication before it was temporarily enjoined by a court injunction). Katherine Graham and her editor are in conflict about whether to take the legal and financial and personal risk to begin publication of the Papers against a President's wishes and a court order. Graham is repeatedly shown in rooms full of men, where she is—apparently—the first woman with her kind of power; and it is clear from her hesitations and nervousness that she is not always confident in her role.

WHEN THE *Post* gets the story—via a copy of the Papers given to a newspaper friend by Ellsberg himself and then transported via its own first-class seat on a plane to Washington—it is confronted with the legal injunction, and a series of meetings about the legal consequences of publishing ensue as the principals of the story move among the offices of the *Post* and the homes of Bradlee and Graham.

More powerfully, we see the words of the story being set into large and heavy type (much more dramatic, of course, than a current word processor and electronic transmission and printing). As in so many films about the press, e.g., *Absence of Malice*, the great scenes are of the long multistory columns of newsprint moving many stories up and down the interior of the *Post* plant once Bradlee tells his printer it's a "go." This is the visual equivalent of the power of the press, whose intellectual force is presumably what Nixon had wished to foreclose. The principals at the

Post go ahead with their actions without certainty, but the philosophical climax to the film comes as we see and hear a newsroom reporter read aloud to others the Supreme Court's 6-3 decision in favor of publication.

DESPITE THIS sense of intellectual and political triumph and moral justification as an effective and definitive climax, the publication of stories about the Papers in 1971 did not end U.S. involvement in Vietnam; the American government continued to support the South Vietnamese government and had some troops there into 1973; the last Americans did not leave until being forced out in 1975, when the government of North Vietnam successfully invaded the South and overran Saigon, thus winning the war and causing all Americans to leave. In other words, the publication of the Papers, while justifiable, did not directly lead to the end of the war, as Daniel Ellsberg had hoped. One could certainly argue that their publication hastened its end.

The "truth" of historical events is far messier than movies; in fact, the opening scenes of *The Post*, set in a Vietnam battle in the early sixties, would lead a third-party observer, I suspect, to no clear conclusion, as a young(er) Ellsberg merely grabs a helmet and goes on a sortie where American forces are ambushed and suffer casualties: that's it. The scenes lack clarity and force; then again, the American government's positions and military strategies could be said, over 20 years, to have suffered from the same confusion. It's a lot easier to focus on a few idealistic reporters and editors and a Supreme Court victory for the First Amendment. A coda scene at the end takes us to the Watergate building and a security guard discovering tape on the locks and an observer noting the inept burglars at the Washington headquarters of the Democratic Party during the key election of 1972.

A knowledgeable viewer is expected to tie this final scene to the entire Watergate scandal, the *Post*'s revelation of it, the key roles of Woodward and Bernstein, and the near-impeachment, then resignation of President Nixon. This was a signal victory for the paper, already highlighted in a memorable film, *All the President's Men*, with its similar scenes of reporters running dramatically through newsrooms. But again, the war went on.

The Future

8. With Both a Bang and a Whimper: *The World's End*

THE WORLD'S END (2013, directed by Edgar Wright) is really two films, a kind of British version of *The Hangover* (2009, with sequels in 2011 and 2013), and a remake of the already once-remade *Invasion of the Body Snatchers* (1956, remade in 1978). Put thus baldly, it hardly seems that those two combined could make a single film, but the film manages to hold it all together by having a single plot narrative that takes five aging British males back to their hometown to recreate the Golden Mile, a pub crawl (12 pubs, 12 pints) they never quite finished at the end of high school. The first part of the film, with its reconsideration of adulthood growth and loss, is the funnier and more interesting. Nevertheless, the filmmaker's original idea incorporated the second strand—that of returning home to the strangeness of homogenized village England, where all the pubs are nearly identical—which became the template for the science fiction part of the film.

The five have long ago parted company since turning 18, and found different life paths: car salesman, real estate agent, contractor, lawyer, and Gary King. You might notice, despite the British locale, that King is not a life path, which is part of the plot and part of the problem. King was the king of the group, now the loser, lost in direction and life, realizing in institutional group therapy that his greatest moment occurred long ago in the epic drunk he and his friends launched 20 years before. By deception and enticement he convinces his aging friends, all since transported from the small town of Newton Haven to London, to join him in another misshapen adventure, even going to the extent of (verbally) killing off his aging mother to win sympathy from the most reluctant, an alienated, distant, plump, and aging teetotaler. As you might predict, Andy the teetotaler begins by ordering only a pint of water, but eventually succumbs under the pressures of the crawl and its attendant aliens to downing five shots of whisky in a row and becoming the most belligerent and aggressive of the pentagroup. We also learn, as the pubs accumulate and the conversation wanders, that two were in love with Sam, a friend's sister, who miraculously also arrives to join the pub crawl.

The musical accompaniment, beginning with a long-lost tape still in King's decaying car, the Beast, is quite original and eventually varies to include a comic march from Kurt Weill and Bertolt Brecht covered by The Doors, a clue to the sophistication and eclecticism of the filmmakers. Even if this film is a kind of failure, it shows a great deal of promise. Like the sound track of 90s songs, the title of each pub is a clue to a point on the crawl's pilgrim's progress.

THE TROUBLE with a 12-pub, 12-pint crawl, is that eventually it becomes even more sodden, more rambling, and more repetitious. There is a folkloric contention among screenwriters that at some point, usually midway, every script "hits the wall." That is, after an original conception and development that seems promising, witty, imaginative, entertaining, it somehow loses focus and questions direction and has no idea where to go—it hits the wall. Good films emerge when writers discover a plausible exit and development plan that emerges from this event. Other films, to those perceptive and attuned to the issue, appear to disintegrate or fail just at this point.

Having created some intriguing characters with genuine life problems and even a bit of wit and intrigue (the quadrangle of two suitors, one brother, one sister for example), the filmmakers decide that the only direction to go is to populate the succeeding pubs with plausible townspeople—suitably dressed and articulate and convincing enough—who turn out to be replacement robots for those left behind by the fabulous five. There is even a discussion of the etymology of the word robot (not once, but three times), which, according to the film, means "slave." ("Robot" was first used in the 1920s Karel Čapek play *RUR*.)

THE ROBOTS here, though seemingly strong, wrestle the real humans forcefully, but can be defeated by pulling off their heads, only to reveal blue stumps, bleeding ink; this decapitation also is the key strategy to tell robot from authentic friend. The ultimate theme of this plot sequence as well as of the *Body Snatchers* films is the modernist fear of identity loss, which is after all the fear that the five have anyway, that they have given up their best selves and retreated into the mediocrity and generalized dissatisfaction of middle-class life and middle age. But the robotization is also a hallmark of what the film repeatedly labels "Starbuckization," where all commercial establishments have been homogenized, made to feel falsely homey. The manic lostness of King, the leader, is merely replicated in the others who, when pushed, reveal the loneliness and suffering of their apparently successful lives. At this point the film gets lost in the plot sequence of the plans of the Network, the vague extraterrestrial power that launches the robots, presumably to make a better universe where everyone is happy; and it deteriorates into a series of futile battles, but ends, sort of, in a climactic scene in a subterranean courtroom bar where the five, two of whom have become robots, confront the voice of the Network, which proves indefensible against the irreverent irrationality of the inebriated.

The Network just gives up!—the first alien power, apparently, to be defeated merely by words, those being the words of two drunken losers defending human independence and irrationality. The Network destroys itself and the remaining bar and apparently all of Newton Haven—there's your bang—leaving the three to be saved by the female member. And this launches us into the dystopic epilogue, where some seem to live in a kind of truncated world, but others find a kind of life. Though this is intriguing, like the right turn the film takes when it goes to robotism, this doesn't make much sense. It does, however, provide a new life for King, now the irreverent hero, apparently, of a resurgent rebel faction in England. The viewpoint has shifted dramatically—since the film began with a prologue from King's point of view, flashing back to high school, but now we hear a voice-over by his antagonistic alter ego Andy Knightley. This film seems to have hit the wall back there, and then gone on, but not to much effect.

9. Echoes of Past and Future:
Oblivion

UTOPIA is the title of a famous 16th century vision by Sir Thomas More that has given its name to visions of a different world. In More, the word is ironic, meaning literally "nowhere"; and it is a place where a seeming ideal state has hidden flaws, such as never fighting war itself, but encouraging war in its allies and subordinates. Samuel Butler echoed this thinking in his *Erewhon*, which is almost Nowhere spelled backwards.

If we consult our databank of images carefully we'll discover it's full of dystopian futures. It's hard to imagine a future constructed out of ideas that isn't dystopian in some way—because the future turns into a fascist state, or because it deteriorates, or because—given its origin—it is the product of a single mind, whether it is Hitler's or Bill Gates's or Ayn Rand's. So many science fiction films incorporate some dystopia at their core because they begin in a vision of the future or a distant world that seems to embody the future. As someone once said, only God creates out of nothing, and so even the future is recognizable as a remolding of the present, and often of our fears in the present. Judging from such films, we fear or anticipate nuclear holocaust, ecological disaster, and the technological eradication of identity—among other disasters. And so at least one purpose of such utopian/dystopian efforts is to confront some of our secret fears.

AND SO, *Oblivion*, the new film with Tom Cruise (directed by Joseph Kosinski), has its attractive/repelling vision of the future. Futurist as it is, like all utopias it is a clone of the present and the past, especially *past films*. The visual landscape is stunning with its clean, ultramodernist architectural and technological lines, and its vast spaces echoing remnants of the world we recognize. Embedded in its visuals and its plot are echoes of many films we have seen over the years, with its decayed and half-buried icons, such as those we remember near the end of *Planet of the Apes* (1968)—of the Empire State Building and perhaps the Golden Gate

Bridge. Of course, Charlton Heston was the star of that film, and intriguingly figured prominently in two other dystopian films of the time that shed some light on *Oblivion*: *Soylent Green* (1973) and *Omega Man* (1971).

In *Soylent Green* the overpopulated world was exhausting useable foodstuffs and the painful secret was that the authorities were killing and reprocessing humans who volunteered due to depression or starvation for euthanasia. These volunteers were reprocessed into a soy slurpy (soylent green) to feed the remaining population. *Omega Man* re-echoes these apocalyptic themes with Heston as one of the last men on an Earth populated essentially by zombies. The biggest problem in these futurist thrillers is, who is the enemy? or how can they be defeated? In *Soylent Green* the enemy is the "them" that surreptitiously kills humans and lies about the food source and assassinates or disappears those who get too close to the truth. This is not so different from *Oblivion*'s ominous Tet spaceship hanging in the day sky. The Tet guides things on the nuclear-devastated Earth, which Jack Harper, Technician #49 (Cruise), living with his female companion Vicka (Victoria, played by Andrea Riseborough), patrols for signs of scav (alien) activity. In *Soylent Green,* most women are concubines referred to derogatorily or dismissively as "furniture," and Tom's companion is a higher-end version of the same. Vicka—dressed elegantly and seductively in a series of neutrally toned skirts and moving about the space-station office in unsensible high heels—offers a communication link, sustenance, and support—when she disrobes smoothly at night to take a dip in the suspended pool and ease Jack's tensions in another way.

This film is also a clone of *Moon* (2009), in which Sam Bell (Sam Rockwell) has a repetitive function as a singular worker on a distant moon. He's only in media contact with "Earth," and in gradually discovering he is a clone he realizes that his "family"—the family he converses with over the airwaves—have been dead for years and were not actually his. This is essentially the self-revelation of Technician 49 when he ventures into the "radiation" zone only to discover another identical version of himself performing a similar task. Like Sam, Jack's memory has been imprinted with scenes from an actual human self and with images of home that represent ceased realities. Jack's dilemma is solved, though, because his remembered wife Julia (Olga Kurylenko) is actually in suspended animation in a crashed spaceship he locates.

OBLIVION offers a stunning world of technology and design: overlaid grids, electronic words, and machines we have not seen before that exist only in digital simulation. Planes sport multi-bendable wings, there are attack drones that look like floating pods with fuel cells and multiple machine guns. Space stations seem to emanate from Disneyland's Tomorrowland designs of years ago. Jack's long-lost girlfriend and wife is mortally wounded but quickly treated and cured with a first-aid spray that stanches the bleeding and heals the wound. And the marvelous Tet itself is reminiscent of so many science fiction space stations, a miniature city cum Pentagon housed in a dramatic geometric shape, vast, alien, and ultimately indifferent. What's amazing, actually, is that there is apparently no one there except the multiple clones of Jack and Vicka preserved in amniotic fluid ready for reissue to needed posts on Earth. The obnoxious and omnipresent Sally (Melissa Leo), who issues directives on video from the Tet, is nowhere to be seen or found on arrival and may simply be a harrowing cinema version of the iPhone's Siri, or may exist only as a digital loop. She may be Jack and Vicka's God but Jack has come to destroy Sally and the Tet.

The echoes of the past are in Jack's memories (not really his own; he is a replicant) of his proposal to Julia, his avatar's wife, in a scene stolen from *A Night to Remember* (1958), where he takes her to the top of the Empire State Building, a part of which remains standing in the current fallen Earthworld. Echoes of earlier humanity and of loss are seen in Jack's treasuring of a passage from Macaulay's *Lays of Ancient Rome*, in the painting *Christina's World*, and in the playing of Procol Harem's *A Whiter Shade of Pale*. Only nostalgia can solve the dilemma of the dystopic future and the robotic self.

At the core of this film is a flimsy plot so common to dystopian movies: when we finally learn what is really going on, it doesn't quite make sense. Jack learns the "scavs" he targets are the only humans left, and that there is no distant colony on a moon of Jupiter, and so he changes allegiance. He and Beech, the scav leader (Morgan Freeman), accept a suicidal mission to destroy the Tet with a miniaturized nuclear device disguised as a drone. The last scene is of Happy Valley on Earth, appropriated from yet another film, with Julia raising—we guess—Jack's offspring and being joined by joyous scavs.

We still wonder—or at least I do—whether the surviving humans have any culture worth preserving or whether they are superior, visually, to the stunning technology that seemed so pure and heartless.

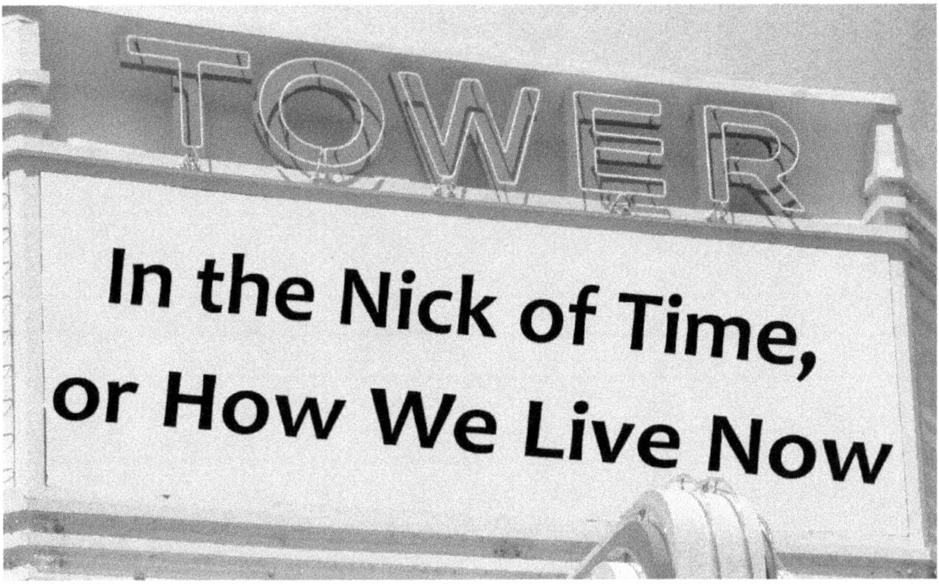
TOWER
In the Nick of Time,
or How We Live Now

10. Indefinite Self-Definition:
Frances Ha

WHO OR what is Frances Ha? That is the question Noah Baumbach's recent film keeps asking and refusing to answer as its central character, Frances Halladay (Greta Gerwig, also its co-writer), moves through a recurring series of relationships and apartments trying to find her way mostly in New York City. And so the film is an attempt to define the amorphous group of young singles from, say, 22 to 30, who have graduated from college and have a series of friends and locations, but are essentially still in limbo or a second latency period.

But Frances's search for self is, for the most part, charming, as she capers about New York City, practicing some dance steps and fake fighting with a friend on a walkway in Central Park. In one scene she runs frenetically in search of an ATM to treat a companion at a restaurant (she had promised, though he offers to pay), finding one at a distance and developing a limp on her way back. A comic, rueful sequence but also a testimony to Frances's integrity and spirit.

The film offers definitions of its central self in terms of a series of locales and relations; in fact, each of its black-and-white styled segments begins with a new address, which marks this pilgrim's progress. In the first one she is living with her college roommate and best friend Sophie, who seems to verge on a lesbian crush, though ultimately is really just her best friend. Frances can't quite make the rent, which is the primary plot motivation for this series of peregrinations. One of her "locales" is a post office box as she spends some summer months as a kind of woodsy counselor at her alma mater, Vassar. (The film is occasionally mildly autobiographical: Gerwig attended Barnard, but Baumbach went to Vassar; Vassar, however, has a conveniently rural setting and serves as a pastoral retreat to the past.)

In another move, also a retreat, Frances moves home to her parents' middle-class house in Sacramento. At one point in the film, Frances claims poverty, but her roommates note that she is really not economically at the bottom of the ladder; and her series of well-heeled friends and relatives essentially establish her as a mildly stressed middle-class bohemian. Nevertheless, she has reached a kind of mild triumph and station of growth when she can afford her own apartment and is beginning to choreograph others' dance routines. In the final sequence she establishes this maturation of self by inserting her name (Frances Ha, truncated from "Halladay" to fit) into the mailbox.

THOUGH PERHAPS the characteristic of this age group in films is a search for romance and success, not nearly in that order, Frances is repeatedly labeled "undatable" by an eligible male friend. This is essentially a comic designation, for Frances is attractive and intriguing, though she continually seems to elude major interest or commitment, just as she can't quite find a permanent job or pay all of her share of the rent. She is not completely formed but shows promise.

Frances's evanescence or search touches lightly on Paris, where she spends a few days on a lark taking advantage of some American acquaintances' pied-a-terre that she heard about at a dinner party the night before. The Parisian jaunt is an accurate gauge of the film's ambivalence. How can a person so stressed for money and unable to pay her share of various rent arrangements afford a two-day stay in Paris? She can't. She charges it on a credit card she just received in the mail. Who does she know in Paris? The only friend isn't answering her phone. How does she feel? A bit disappointed, lonely, and sad. Yet, despite appearances, it is not a disaster, just part of the process. Frances is much more saddened when she hears of Sophie's engagement to Patch, a trader at Goldman Sachs, and their move to Japan; but Sophie never deserts Frances, doesn't marry the fiancé, and returns to the U.S., where she appears to have a substantial job at a major publisher.

THIS FILM marks one of several by Baumbach that are essentially character studies, particularly of eccentric characters who are not quite loveable. Perhaps the most famous of these is *The Squid and the Whale*, in which both divorcing parents are a bit troubling or nasty, though the film is essentially a portrait of the emergence from adolescence that the parents' split occasions in the children. In *Greenberg* two years ago, the central character (Ben Stiller) was just recovering from a mental-health hospitalization and trying to recapture his distant past in Los Angeles while house-sitting for his far more successful brother. We watched Greenberg disintegrate in a series of conversations with people who might offer him friendship or affection, but he did not quite proceed to self-destruction. Gerwig played second fiddle in that film, as his occasional girlfriend Dolores. None of these characters seem gainfully employed, though they are conveniently surrounded (and supported) by members of the upper middle class.

Though these films might not have clear direction or message, they offer a kind of honesty and directness that the typical Hollywood film lacks—especially because their development and their outlines are unpredictable. *Frances Ha* has the charm, originality, and honesty that a more typical Hollywood romantic comedy or summer blockbuster special-effects film lacks.

11. Not a Sequel, but a Look Backward: *Return of the Secaucus 7*

IT OPENS with the unclogging of a toilet and ends with a young man furiously chopping wood—two seemingly quotidian chores that try to express more, and are yet appealing, understandable, resonant. *Return of the Secaucus 7* (1980, directed by John Sayles) suggests a sequel to a film we've never seen, but is actually best understand as a poor man's answer to *The Big Chill* (1983, directed by Lawrence Kasdan). And now, in 2012, it's a doubly nostalgic film, reminiscent of the counterculture, quasi-revolutionary 1970s, when many of us grew up or maintained that we grew up, and also reminiscent of the 1980s, when it was set and made, when we supposedly matured from that revolutionary period.

The occasion is a reunion, in Vermont, of the seven people who were arrested in Secaucus, New Jersey, ten years before, capriciously, on their return from a political rally in the nation's capital. The arrested created a community of friends, which has since renewed its vows several times at these annual reunions. Stop here if you don't want to learn key plot data.

And so the film is an exploration of social trends and changes, and an examination of the maturation process, and, as most good films are, a confrontation with American values. There is a history lesson on the Haymarket strikes; also a hilarious disquisition by an aspiring physician, on why you should "never leave home without" a birth control device, and a variety of scenes that are episodic and occasionally lame, but still amusing and unpredictable. Other topics covered sporadically are the music of rock and roll, how much of a sellout working in politics may be, whether teaching high school has any intellectual or political value, and the ethics of a hookup with your best friend's girl.

What distinguishes *Return* from *Chill* is the lack of superficial success and the apparent lack of arrogance of all the major figures. In *The Big Chill* we have stars as actors, Jeff Goodman, Kevin Kline, Glenn Close, Mary Kay Place, William Hurt. We have stars as characters: a reporter for *People* magazine, millionaire owners of a major shoe company (perhaps like Nike), a Washington staffer. Everyone in *Chill* seems a member of the 1%, and yet most are unhappy or dissatisfied or unfulfilled, while remaining witty and attractive and compelling—it's a certain kind of American film, of which there are many. John Sayles's *Return of the Secaucus 7*, by contrast, had no recognizable actors, and its characters were not stars, and it seemed shot, as it was, over a few weeks on a modest budget in a small town. The characters in Sayles's film were high school teachers, an actress in summer stock, a struggling guitar player, drug counselors, and—with a slight contrast—two aides to a senator.

There's a modest revision to the comment "no recognizable actors," and this is part of the charm of returning to such a film after many years, like recognizing Richard Dreyfuss as having a 2-word bit part in *The Graduate* when you see it twenty years later. A few of the apparent nonentities have become entities and their film debuts now seem intriguing, even charming. The most well-known is David Strathairn, now a veteran of many A-list films and currently playing William Seward opposite Daniel Day Lewis's Lincoln; he debuted as a minor character in Sayles's film, not one of the 7, but a townie gas station employee who seemed to chew up the scenery whenever he was on screen and even walked backward over a parked car while chatting up the budding doctor. Some of you may also recognize Gordon Clapp, who went on to a role in *NYPD Blue*.

The film keeps asking the question, what becomes of youthful idealism and incipient revolution, and what arcs do lives defined by mobility and some college take? At some level, it confronts one of the perennial questions in narrative and poetry: loss, or what to make of a diminished thing. It offers no answers, and it doesn't have the conventional drive of an American film with plot or resolution, but it also speaks with its own earnest authenticity and charm.

12. A Stillness at the Center: *Manchester by the Sea*

MANCHESTER BY THE SEA, starring Casey Affleck, Ben's younger brother, is a superb film, the best I've seen all year and, in fact, in some time. And that's as far as you should read here if you haven't already seen (and want to see) it, because the rest of what you'll find here will tell you a great many things about what happens and what's key in the film.

I'm really tired, as you might surmise, of film appreciations or reviews or previews that promise to withhold the key details that spoil your experience of the film; they always betray that promise to some degree. The better the film, the more any pre-disclosed detail somewhat spoils it for a first-time viewer. It's like making love for the first time to someone you're really excited about, only somebody hands you a guidebook as you enter the bedroom alerting you to key moments and what to look out for. Well, it's not really like that, but I hope you get the idea.

So, what's so great about this film? Probably that it doesn't neatly fit into some pre-established type or popular genre or demographic—it's not about race, and it's not about some dystopian future, and it's not about a great historical event that we're all familiar with but don't know well, and it's not for young lovers, and it doesn't have the sort of happy ending that Woody Allen has said so many of his producers encouraged him to add to films to make them more profitable or salable—yet somehow Allen has continued to make films and profits. In other words, it's about realistic people in a human place experiencing pain, suffering, loss, and a variety of emotions.

It's also understated, with the emotion most of the time repressed, hidden, beneath the surface, disguised.

THE FILM'S opening scene, like its title, is inviting and misleading, even bland. Why do they occasionally name films after places in an anodyne, anonymous way? Like *Philadelphia*? Of course, Philadelphia is the city of brotherly love, by translation from the Greek, but then what of *The Philadelphia Story?* By contrast *Tinker Tailor Soldier Spy* is at once a quasi-nursery rhyme, a conundrum, and a plot summary. *Zero Dark Thirty* is powerfully mysterious and military and is ultimately explained, briefly, in the dialog. *12 Years a Slave* is simultaneously an eloquent plot summary and an indictment and a puzzle. *Boyhood* adroitly sums up a key era as well as a cinematic strategy. Perhaps *Gallipoli* is the intriguing exception, both a place name and a reference to a classic, tragic piece of early twentieth century history.

In *Manchester by the Sea* we see a moment of witty and engaging horseplay on a fishing boat between Casey (Lee Chandler) and his perhaps eight-year-old nephew, Patrick, as Patrick's father, Joe, the boat's captain, jokes menacingly about throwing young boys to schools of sharks.

We soon see Lee in a landlocked environment, Boston, shoveling snow outside a building, then discussing minor repairs with tenants in a variety of settings. He seems like the Lee of the opening sequence; he is thoughtful, accurate, helpful, but often noncommittal. Perhaps a bit terse, reserved, not as human, playful, as engaged as he had been with his nephew. He appears pretty much the same Lee, well-built, handsome, definitely attractive. One female tenant goes to another room and talks audibly if not quite indiscreetly with a girlfriend about the crush she has on her handyman, wondering if it's a hindrance that he's doing plumbing maintenance on her shit-laden toilet. While he's fixing a chandelier, an older woman kvetches on the phone about attending a grandchild's bat mitzvah. A younger woman in a negligee, in another bathroom, argues with Lee about the source of leaked water, and eventually the conversation deteriorates to adjectival fuckings, though no fucking is done.

Again, Lee is shoveling more snow, same location, similar Sisyphean positioning, though the photography and the editing don't overtly comment in this way at all. Later in a bar having a drink by himself next to two attractive women, Lee has beer spilled on him, the female spiller apologizes, a flirtatious moment to which he responds eventually only by throwing punches at the two suit-and-tied men across from him at the bar.

Something is missing in Lee, something hidden, something subterranean. But we don't know what; we don't even recognize that his verbal offering is subdued. If we thought about it, we might wonder that a man who had seemed to enjoy children has no interactions with them, and that he is subtly avoiding deeper interactions with the opposite sex. In fact, pretty much with anybody. He lives in a sublevel single room through which two higher windows provide the only light.

EVENTUALLY a cellphone call summons Lee out of this subterranean hell into a lighter place, Manchester (Massachusetts), where his older brother Joe has just died of a heart attack and left Lee as the now-16-year-old Patrick's guardian. The attack may seem sudden but we see a slowback (not a flashback) to a scene years earlier where Joe is diagnosed with congestive heart failure and given a prognosis of perhaps ten years; the three men in the room (Joe, Lee, and their father) joke a bit, but Joe's wife walks out abruptly, leaving him there. What seems sudden is never sudden; catastrophe always has its Cassandras.

THE SLOWBACKS are clues, keys to the subterranean life. Interspersed with this Manchester narrative—the present of Joe's death and its aftermath, mostly shots of the harbor, ships slowly moving, or gulls hovering above, stately houses seen on a headland—are shots of Lee's backstory with his family. Actually, the gulls and boats are pretty much all that are seen moving—despite its village setting and the life of the sea, virtually no human beings are distinguishable in Manchester. Manchester is bucolic, idyllic, a series of set landscapes and seascapes that are, simply, beautiful. At variance with this setting is the human life we learn about in the other scenes—painful, tragic, barely utterable.

As Lee and Patrick go through the rounds of uncle-nephew duties following Joe's death—they visit mortuary, lawyer, ultimately the funeral service—we gradually learn more of both their backgrounds. And in between we see their interaction at Patrick's home as Lee temporarily plays the role of parent, approving sleepovers by Patrick's girlfriend, giving him money for food, maintaining his stance that he won't move from Boston. Again, something is unvisited, unsaid. Lee's conversation is not catatonic, but it is not thoroughly warm or jovial, and his responses are full of polite refusals, declines of invitations to dinner or socialization. In one scene Patrick tries to convince his uncle to come into his girlfriend's house because her mother is interested in Lee; he is resistant, but eventually acquiesces. The conversation between Lee and the mother is so barren and under-responsive that she eventually flees to her daughter's bedroom and pleas for rescue, comically interrupting the younger generation's attempts at sexual satisfaction.

But Lee had a wife; she is mentioned as one person to notify of Joe's death. We see her in one sequence where he comes home and plays with their children and climbs onto her in bed, as she resists because she has a cold. Why is he now so clueless with women?

THE FILM'S climactic scene is an unspoken sequence accompanied by a beautiful classical piece by Albinoni, set in flashbacks against Lee's visits to lawyer, priest. The scene begins with a mildly drunken ping pong party of Lee and male friends, the only time in the film we see him congenial and happy among a group of peers. It is 2 a.m., and his wife interrupts. In the breakup of the party, Lee trudges across snow-ridden shortcuts to a convenience store, trudges home to encounter his house on fire and his wife being taken to an ambulance on a stretcher. Three small black bags emerge eventually from the smoking ruin. They echo, in mute and mysterious silence, the three framed objects Lee removes from his subterranean Boston basement and resets on his bureau in his temporary Manchester residence. We never see the photos in the frames. We never see the bodies of the children. We don't need to.

A related scene, a powerful emotional climax underplayed for what is not shown, not said, is a late encounter on the streets of Manchester between Lee and his ex-wife Randi. It is accidental, it is unexpected, it is heartbreaking, and I cried both times I saw it. Again, it is a case of a woman making an overture to Lee, a request simply to have lunch together, which he rejects, with polite avoidance. Randi is all forgiveness, apologies, and love for the unspoken tragedy between them.

The pain is real, but so much is not shown. Lee's is not, of course, the only suffering in the film. His nephew has also experienced painful loss: his mother, mysteriously unavailable for some time, was an alcoholic, and banned from the family. When she welcomes her son to her new home and new husband for a meal, there is distance and tension under the surface. Lee understands his nephew's pain, his disinterest in living again with his mother. However, Lee himself admits he cannot see a way back. This vague line encompasses so much of what he has repressed, of his own loss and guilt, of his inability to move forward usefully; he can have an interlude back in Manchester, the scene of his early boyhood and young fatherhood and ultimate catastrophe, but he cannot stay. It is so painful that Lee returns to Boston, to another janitorial job.

But this time the room he rents will have a space for Patrick: Lee experiences great pain because he cares. Patrick's suffering is disguised and allayed by the surface pleasures of late adolescence: school, friends, a band of which he is a leader, his hoped-for future as owner of his father's fishing boat. But Patrick does break down, once from the strain, suffering a panic attack when deluged by frozen chicken from the refrigerator, reminding him of his father lingering in a freezer awaiting a spring burial in more accessible ground. Lee's response on the occasion of the panic attack shows the love and parenting skills he retains, offering Patrick an ear, refusing to leave his bedroom until he is satisfied the young man is okay. When uncle and nephew later visit an ominous gun rack in the family house, and Patrick asks whether the guns are for Lee to kill himself or to shoot Patrick, Lee explains that they can be sold to buy Patrick a new motor for his boat. Remembered angst and suffering are always available, but renewed tragedy can be avoided.

The movie lingers on its final scene, Lee and Patrick fishing off the back of the boat Patrick has now inherited, an echo of the film's opening sequence, a kind of closure without renewal or resurrection. The end credits linger over the stillness of Manchester's elegiac exteriors; the only moving or animated objects are seagulls and a lone duck.

13. Why Does Jasmine Have the Blues?
Blue Jasmine

WOODY ALLEN'S recent film, *Blue Jasmine*, is his best in the last decade, perhaps a return to the heights of emotionally and intellectually challenging films like *Hannah and Her Sisters* (1986) and *Crimes and Misdemeanors* (1989). Its title is both name and comment on its central character, played powerfully yet subtly by Cate Blanchett: a character whose given name was Jeanette Francis, but who changed it, like Woody Allen (né Allen Konigsberg) himself changed his, to alter her sense of herself, to create a new identity.

But we see her in mid-life and mid-flight as her identity has begun to fall apart; in fact, we see her first on a plane talking to a companion who appears to be a relative, and Jasmine is elegantly dressed and appears well-to-do. But like the artificial shot of the plane itself that begins the film, all this is facade. She is not what she seems, and we are constantly trying to figure out just who she is. She has flown to San Francisco to live with her sister Ginger, an analogue or a foil for herself, as the sisters in Allen's *Hannah* are for each other. The other passenger on the plane, whom Jasmine seems so intimate with, actually doesn't know Jasmine and is glad to be rid of her at Baggage Claim; it's clear that Jasmine talks a lot, about herself, and unfortunately occasionally just to herself, but as if someone else were there. The Louis Vuitton baggage she arrives with and the first-class seat she occupies conflict dramatically with her status as a bankrupt with large debts to the government.

Jasmine and Ginger are actually not biological sisters, both being adopted by the same parents, but both are still searching for themselves and for economic security and social status that would help them define their identities.

JASMINE APPEARED to have found this identity in her husband, Hal (Alec Baldwin). Scenes of the two of them continue to intercut with the present motion of the film to give us both background and a sense of

Jasmine's intense memories and regrets. Her self-designating name suggests she is attractive, elegant, and also a bit ephemeral or shallow. She is whisked away from college and any pretense of profession by Hal's allure: wealth and pedestalization. Despite a few signs that his financier's wealth may edge against the legal limits, she remains quite pleased with him, especially as he brings diamond trinkets to her in her bubble bath. Hal is one of those figures we have become familiar with in a series of recent films following the fiscal implosion of 2008, from Richard Gere in *Arbitrage* (2012) to Jeremy Irons in *Margin Call* (2011).

The intercuts trace the gradual decline of the Jasmine-Hal relationship and the recurrent evasion of reality necessary for Jasmine to maintain her status: she elides Hal's discussion of financial evasions and represses a variety of forms of evidence that indicate he is having affairs, one of which Ginger observes in vestige but does not communicate. The climax is the revelation that he plans to marry the au pair, and Jasmine's reaction (a call to the FBI) reveals that she has intuited his financial manipulations for a long time but has ignored them as long as he preserved her other illusions. Hal is not only arrested and convicted but commits suicide in prison.

Jasmine's illusions and decay are underlined by her pill-popping of Xanax and her swilling of Stoli Vodka direct from the bottle. When reality closes in, we see her periodically holding conversations with an imaginary interlocutor, and those around her begin to look at her strangely. But in this film, surfaces are frequently compelling, and Jasmine continues to dress in Chanel and appears classy enough to attract her San Francisco employer, a dentist, who puts the make on her in the office. She finds him gauche and unappealing. She is attracted to appealing surfaces, so later she falls for the younger, attractive diplomat with a beautiful new home in Marin and an impressive background.

Still devoted to surfaces, she glamorizes her own past with a decorator's license and a deceased husband who is *not* a suicidal criminal. When her lies and her past—simultaneously in the form of Ginger's ex-husband, Augie—catch up with her, she is doubly unmasked and deserted by her new diplomat lover on the verge of buying her an engagement ring.

Bereft as Ginger reunites with boyfriend Chili, whom she had rejected under Jasmine's tutelage, Jasmine is left alone on a park bench, extremely well-dressed and still in dialog with herself.

THIS TALE of two sisters is also a tale of two cultures that inevitably intermingle—the 1% and the 99%, the poor and the rich. The film appears to strike a blow for the poor, who may be struggling and gauche, as in Ginger's ex-husband Augie and her new lover Chili—but they appear to be earnest and honest and love her. That's of course an oversimplification, but not by much.

14. Love and Death in Two Films: *Amour* and *Silver Linings Playbook*

ROMEO AND JULIET condenses two of literature's great themes, love and death, in the liebestod of romantic young love, leaving both lovers beautifully and tragically dead before they reach 20. Most of us survive young love and our 20s and have gone on to watch a zillion movies that may be loosely designated romantic comedies. The romantic comedy may be one of Hollywood's most successful formats, but a viewer easily tires of it or turns to sterner fare. This year *Amour* and *Silver Linings Playbook*, both nominated for Oscars for best actress and best film, discovered a new twist on this perennial motif. See them absolutely, but if you like surprises, you should stop reading *here*.

HEMINGWAY WROTE that if two people are in love it will not end well, because one will die first. His *Romeo and Juliet*, combining love and war, was *Farewell to Arms*. But *Amour* (2012, directed by Michael Haneke and winner of the Oscar for best foreign-language film), despite its promising title of Love, doesn't quite take that route because it explores the eventual painful and excruciating death as an aging couple confronts the mental and physical deterioration of one of the partners as the other—in increasing isolation in their elegant, comfortable, and confining Parisian apartment—tries to care for her. We are shown so much that we would rather not see or not imagine, and the metteur-en-scène keeps showing us the disconcerting side of scenes that upset our expectations. We begin, for example, with the end. Firemen and other last responders break into a sealed set of rooms only to discover an elegantly clad aging female body lying on a bed surrounded by flowers. And the rest of the film simply—or not so simply—tells us what led up to that scene.

Amour is remarkable for several defamiliarizing scenes, including the second one, where we watch an audience watching. And we're waiting and trying to figure out what's going on. Later we see patches of some impressionist landscapes, and again, we're uncertain. Are these the paintings on the walls of the Parisian apartment? Apparently not. These destabilizing elements reveal an integrated and meaningful artistic life and marriage breaking down under the pressures of mental disintegration, as in an early breakfast scene in which the wife just freezes and can't talk and doesn't seem to respond: the first clue the couple has that their love is now threatened by disintegration and death.

This Parisian couple has had a life together in music, playing the piano, instructing talented young students; their daughter is married, unhappily, to a musician. But the wife's disintegration is not pretty or musical or artistic. Her left side is paralyzed by a stroke, her speech disintegrates and eventually disappears; she becomes at times little more than an animate object, illuminated by the sense there is someone within. We watch her fed reluctantly or unwillingly by nurse and husband, watch her nude, being bathed upright in the shower—these are not the glamorous scenes of romance or sex that we usually associate with French films, or that the actors themselves starred in during their youth (Jean-Louis Trintignant in *A Man and a Woman*, Emmanuelle Riva in *Hiroshima mon amour*). The grimaces Emmanuelle Riva evokes around the mouth and shoulders are painful, excruciating, and among the reasons she was nominated for an acting award. Music arrives now only in snatches, conversations, and memories—a beautiful respite for the audience as we hear snatches of Bach, of a Beethoven "Bagatelle" and other pieces. But neither art nor love nor the daughter provides much balm for the unrelenting end of life. The husband is patient, caring; the wife is frequently resentful or lost in her world or even suicidal. Hemingway was right: this cannot end well. We see the process that leads to the end, to the not particularly imaginative way the husband administers euthanasia. When *Amour* is gone, we are left with mystery, but also with sympathy and the recognition of a painful truth about love.

IN SHAKESPEARE, tragedies often end with multiple bodies littering the stage, comedies with multiple simultaneous marriages. As we shift from *Amour* to *Silver Linings Playbook* (2012, directed by David O. Russell and the winner of the Oscar for best actress in a leading role— Jennifer Lawrence), we move from the tragedy of love to its comedy or possibility. Yet *Playbook* is hardly your typical romantic comedy, because it begins, as *Amour* ends, in mutual loss. Pat Solitaro, the male half of the film's romantic couple (played by Bradley Cooper), is first seen in a mental institution, and he is suffering from bipolar disorder. Mental illness here is a convenient trope, but the dramatization of bipolar disorder doesn't fit the medical conventions of the disease, and the star's psychiatrist unprofessionally socializes with him at a football game and comes to his home; but hey, it's Hollywood. Pat is estranged from his wife, who had been having an affair with a colleague; Pat had attacked the colleague mercilessly, been sent by the justice system to a mental institution, and now his mother's care. Pat has lost wife, job, house, personal freedom, and social respect: many acquaintances and neighbors flee him when he approaches. Another aging adolescent relegated to living with her parents, Tiffany Maxwell (Lawrence) is also suffering romantic loss, after her policeman husband died suddenly and unexpectedly: she adopted a project of going to bed with everyone at work, including the women. The two not only suffer from emotional distress, they are incautiously outspoken and direct, and often hilarious. Despite Pat's obsession with his estranged wife and (illegal) attempts to reunite with her, we sense that these two are both seeking replacements for lost love.

Pat's extreme behavior is first shown when he expels Hemingway's *Farewell to Arms* from his attic room via a closed window because the ending disappoints him; it doesn't fit his need for romantic fulfillment, since Catherine Barkley dies in childbirth. It is 4 a.m.; nevertheless, Pat also goes immediately to his parents' bedroom to complain. The outrageous behavior here is essentially comic, though it would clearly be disruptive and disturbing in a real family. We love and are amused by these outrageous scenes in films; in "real life" it would be painful to live with them in our lovers or our family or our neighborhood.

Eventually the audience realizes that Pat and Tiffany are moving much closer to each other emotionally, a fairly typical pattern for a romantic comedy where the initial participants are seen as antagonists. After all, they do have something in common—their illnesses—and in another comic scene at a dinner party they discuss, quite astutely, the emotional and physical effects of the various pharmacopeia they have ingested and occasionally rejected. So, despite logic, realism, society, and statistical likelihood, according to the dictates of the genre, they are both physically attractive and therefore made for each other. Hollywood romantic comedy tends to bend the curve of human likelihood to satisfy our popcorn needs.

In addition to their underlying attraction, the relationship of Pat and Tiffany is built further on a kind of occupational therapy as they work together in Tiffany's studio to perfect a couples' dance routine, a sequence that extends over weeks and is tied artfully together by a cut from Dylan and Cash singing "Girl from the North Country Fair." Their burgeoning affair, seemingly unbeknownst to Pat, transcends the reservations of their watchful parents with whom they each, severally, live. In a memorable comic scene, Tiffany defends her influence on Pat and the family's Philadelphia obsession with the Eagles in an artful, surprising, and comic demonstration of her knowledge of football scores, lore, and even the state motto of New York. Ultimately the film, albeit unconvincingly and unrealistically, is a portrayal of illness rescued (and cured) by love. The climax, at the dance contest for which Tiffany had convinced Pat to prepare, entwines all the film's themes in a trifecta of success—for Pat's transcendence over his doomed obsession with his estranged wife, for his father's seemingly doomed bets and bookie business, for the relation of Pat and Tiffany.

ONE FILM, the romantic comedy, ends well; the other doesn't. Each has found a new artistic twist on the perennial subject of love.

15. Dubious Urban Mythologies:
Broken City
and
Gangster Squad

SO, A few weeks after New Year's, we have two police films with old themes set in the two traditional American urban police meccas, New York and Los Angeles, though parts of the first were apparently shot in Louisiana, which has superior skyscrapers and had a former mayor under indictment, and that is what eventually happens to the New York mayor in *Broken City*. One way of thinking about film, other than wondering how faithfully it replicates the book on which it was based, is to think of it in terms of genres. These two, more or less, fit the cop genre, which arguably has replaced the Western genre, which reached its apogee in the 1950s, and began to be "revised" in the 1970s (think *Butch Cassidy and the Sundance Kid*, *McCabe and Mrs. Miller*) before it dwindled to almost nothing in the current era.

What cop and Western genre have in common is violence, an absolutist sense of right and wrong mixed in with a mythology about what is otherwise a series of real events and places. At the center is a redeeming and noble figure who enforces the law or at least justice. Underlying the Western was often a hidden eschatology of religious transcendence, as for example, when Shane ascends into the mountains at the end, a kind of Christlike martyr to the violence and inequality of Western economics and politics.

The cop film, unlike the Western, has a much more tenuous hold on mythology as its viewers live in the place and era virtually contemporary with events that often seem all too real, while the Western is about a historical moment and place so vaguely understood by most viewers that myths about it can prevail. The urban landscape of cop films indulges in mythologies that become dubious, as in the current two films under consideration.

The Los Angeles of *Gangster Squad* (directed by Ruben Fleischer) was a real place, a post-World War II melange of returned soldiers, boosterism, entrepreneurship, and, in this case, invading gangsters from the East, like Mickey Cohen. (The East as a place of corruption was also an underlying motif of many Westerns, juxtaposed against the supposed virtues of magnificence and eternity of Western landscapes.) Cohen survived his time in LA and eventually died in his sleep in his 70s, though you'd never guess this from the film, which has a kind of gunfight at the OK Corral shootout as a climax. But its team of cops-turned-gangster-exterminators is admirably varied, with a returned World War II veteran, an idealist with surprising motivations, a Western six-shooter specialist, his Hispanic sidekick, and a communications expert. The success of their exploits is pretty much mythological, as when five of them endure a cordon of numerous thugs with machine guns protecting Mickey in a downtown hotel.

The series of confrontations and shootouts does build up the suspense, and the portrayal of Cohen by Sean Penn is extraordinary, as a supreme narcissist who thinks he is God and has misbehaving subordinates torn apart by two automobiles, as if we have returned not to the violence of the old West, but to the drawn-and-quartered punishments of much earlier times. Other historical figures from Los Angeles and the late forties emerge, such as Thomas Parker, the police chief at the time, and Darryl Gates, chief of a latter era. No one in the film seems particularly disturbed by the fact that the squad, composed of policemen, violates everyone's civil rights and a series of laws and doesn't arrest criminals, but assassinates them.

THE NEW YORK of *Broken City* (directed by Allen Hughes) replicates the urban atmosphere of a number of films where the mayor is thoroughly corrupt and slick, despite the fact that New York's last four mayors (Bloomberg, Giuliani, Dinkins, Koch) have been rarely accused of corruption. This is quite a transformation, as if the evil cattle baron of the Western in historical fact had been a peaceable vegetarian sheepherder. But the mayor's corruption here seems to be a given of the genre. The retired cop Billy Taggart (Mark Wahlberg), is befriended by and hired by the mayor and then becomes entangled in a plot of assassination, lies, and fiscal corruption. Aside from its lack of contemporary plausibility, the explanation for the corruption seems farfetched and an accident of script. It's a bit like a failed McGuffin, a term originated by Alfred Hitchcock to describe a mysterious piece of information that the protagonist and the audience are searching for throughout a film (e.g., what is the meaning of "the 39 steps"?), but by the end we don't much care about it, and it's largely irrelevant to what we have learned about human behavior and politics.

THE MCGUFFIN in *Broken City* is an unconvincing and unsatisfying motivator. Here Mayor Hostetler (Russell Crowe) is unconvincing in his performance as a manipulator and corrupter. He gets $4 billion for the city from the sale of some apartment towers, which eases its financial problems, even if it may displace poor renters; his wife is unfaithful, but he is apparently chaste. He initially helps Billy as a policeman avoid a guilty verdict because it wouldn't be good for the city, but Billy is required to resign from the force. In the film's main action Hostetler has hired Billy as a private detective to look into his wife's affairs (pun intended). Somewhere here, especially in the estrangement from his wife and his use of political/violent manipulatives, Hostetler seems to echo, albeit dimly, the monster portrayed as the mayor of Chicago in the Starz TV series *Boss*. But that boss is a true monster and he's hiding urban pollution of massive proportions and he betrays his own daughter and his staff and his anointed successor and is also suffering from a terminal illness and some form of temporary dementia. And he comes from a city we have in the past associated with highhanded political manipulation and many forms of corruption. But Hostetler has to be corrupt and manipulative, apparently, to make this genre work.

As the layers are pealed back we learn the mayor was trying to suppress information. What information? Something about those apartment towers. They were sold to another company. Yet a third company was involved in the transaction, but it's not clear exactly what they do or why they will get the majority of the profit. In the revelation of the McGuffin, it turns out the mayor was an officer in that third company, and that explains his use of Billy, his assassination of his opponent's campaign manager, and everything. Huh? Like most McGuffins, this is also revealed so quickly that we are not to question its logic or practicality, or even why it took the mayor seven years to become so venal (apparently he's angling for an unprecedented third term, which Bloomberg was able to achieve, but no one suspects Bloomberg was corrupt, because he started political life as a gazillionaire).

Even less convincing is the variety of motivations of those surrounding the mayor. Billy is vouchsafed many revelations by his police chief, who seems only a shade less corrupt and manipulative than his putative boss; and he's actually the one having the affair with the mayor's wife (Catherine Zeta-Jones), though we don't see the two even interested in each other. Jack Valliant (Barry Pepper), the mayor's opponent in the election, never appears sincere and offers only vague alternatives to the policies of Hostetler—even though he's supposed to be the political white knight who will save the city, from what?

The mythologies multiply in Billy's behavior as private eye and police enforcer. He beats up or threatens everyone, even innocent parties. When Valliant's campaign manager is found dead outside an apartment, the police arrive and Valliant is discovered hiding inside. He's questioned by the police chief and Billy (who, after all, has no official status at this point) and seems embarrassed and reticent. Billy repairs to a bathroom and starts running water in the tub; eventually he takes Valliant there and offers him the urban cop-private eye version of water boarding. To find out what? That Valliant is gay, that he wouldn't defend his lover and friend, and that the campaign manager had something on the mayor. When Valliant divulges this information, he is quite congenial and comfortable with Billy, not seeming to be at all resentful or fearful of someone who had just tried to drown him. But the scene makes no sense to me, except to show Billy is relentless in pursuit of the truth. What's so startling about a gay figure in a mayoral election in 2012, especially in New York, where one of the mayoral candidates this year is a lesbian? Even less plausible, what's so strange about a candidate and his campaign manager meeting in an apartment? Valliant's reticence is just inexplicable, except as an excuse for an exercise in pseudo-police brutality. To me he seems guilty of nothing except inexplicable silence and reticence, which justify a near-drowning to extract a non-confession?

Other characters in this movie just don't seem to act like the human beings I know, which might be excused if it were set in a foreign country or were *Star Trek*, or if I were a hermit. Billy's attractive live-in girlfriend of seven years, Natalie Barrow, breaks up with him one evening out because he goes off the wagon one night and starts drinking heavily. It's over, like that, no moving out, no phone calls, no lingering discussion. Well, I supposed that could explain why Billy's interrogation technique is so brutal. We never see or hear from his love again, though Katy Bradshaw—his secretary, girl-of-all-work, and bill collector, and the only character in the film with heart—does offer some hope when she hands him a gift at film's end, a phone card, so he can call her from prison.

Maybe the problem here is that this is a film without heroes or anyone worthy of admiration, conviction, or a vote. Billy does make the self-sacrificial gesture at the end, so the evil mayor (Hostetler) can be defeated. But up to that point Billy was merely a directionless private detective with a penchant for violence. The only thing broken at the end of *Broken City* is your heart, that films of such little conviction and imagination are actually made by such talented actors and directors.

Art

16. Psycho Revisited, or Adultery v. Art: *Hitchcock*

IF YOU'RE a film buff or if you have nothing to do this weekend, or if you're a fan of Alfred Hitchcock, or if you wanted to know how *Psycho* was made, but were too afraid to ask, you might want to spend a few hours watching the 2012 film, *Hitchcock,* directed by Sacha Gervasi.

It's based on a book-length study by Stephen Rebello, *Alfred Hitchcock and the Making of Psycho*, first published in 1990. The film's frame is intriguing, as Hitchcock at its beginning and end addresses us directly about what we are about to see and what we have seen; though clearly the man himself is dead and is being played by Anthony Hopkins in a fat suit. One of the troubles with movies like these is that, despite their various claims to authenticity, we know that they are in fact fake. Anthony Hopkins doesn't really look like Hitch, though he has Hitchcock's pauses and speech down to a T; actually, the actor Godfrey Teale in *Hitchcock*'s *39 Steps* looks a lot more like Franklin D. Roosevelt (as he is supposed to) than Hopkins looks like Hitchcock, or Helen Mirren looks like Alma Reville (actually, she looks far more attractive), or Scarlett Johansson looks like Janet Leigh, or the nearly anonymous actor James D'Arcy looks like a squirrelly Tony Perkins, who played the murderer in *Psycho*.

An NPR program quoted a recent Hitchcock biographer's critique of errors of fact in the film—that Hitchcock didn't really have to mortgage his house to get Paramount to commit to the picture, that the Hitchcocks actually had a sound, 50-year marriage, that Hitchcock didn't actually try to terrorize Janet Leigh in the shower scene.

But for me none of these is the point, especially since the biographer himself seems to be evasive on some of the key facts. The film presents both Hitchcocks as toying with infidelity, with Alfred peering through keyholes at his voluptuous actresses, and being angered that Vera Miles gave up her career to pursue domesticity and motherhood, and with Alma as co-writing a screenplay with an old family friend who seems to be making a pass at her. It also presents them never crossing over the line and offering accolades to each other for their loyalty as well as their cinematic excellence. Nevertheless, in the 1980s Donald Spoto created a mild firestorm in his Hitchcock biography (*The Dark Side of Genius*) with his tales of Hitchcock lusting after some of his blonde stars, and actually suggesting to Tippi Hedren a dream of undying love. *Hitchcock*'s blend of quasi-adulterous material underlying the filming of *Psycho* thus has some basis in titillating fact (a pun Hitchcock himself makes anent Leigh's physique) and does enliven the idea of the intercourse between art and life.

But the film also cheapens the idea of how art is made, suggesting that Hitchcock's primary impulse is audience manipulation and suspense. Both the actual film and the film that is its subject matter reach a climax of sorts in the shower scene, as when it portrays Hitch himself standing outside the auditorium door to conduct, in a series of gratifying knife stabs, the audience's screams as the actress in *Psycho* is attacked in the shower scene. So, the purpose of all this manipulation is merely momentary and illusory gasping; this is unfair to Hitchcock in a major sense, since his films from *The 39 Steps* to *North by Northwest* to *The Birds* offer a series of commentaries on many profound issues, such as the nature of identity and the fragility of human society. *Hitchcock*, on the other hand, seems like so many American movies to be about the well-known and expected success when a master of suspense manipulates an actress and an audience and makes a fortune.

17. The Ungreat Gatsby, a Failed Attempt to Transmit Literature to Film: *The Great Gatsby*

WHY DOES anyone want to do yet another film version of one of the great American novels of the twentieth century? The answer, I suppose, is the same as why anyone tries to climb mountains: because they are there. Actually, despite the relatively small fatality rate, there is far more repeat success climbing mountains than there is any significant success turning great literature into even moderately successful or satisfying films. In fact, the effort is littered with the near-dead bodies of failed attempts at great fiction-to-film transformations.

Melville's *Moby Dick*? Often thought to be the great American novel of the nineteenth century—an eminently forgotten 1956 attempt starring Gregory Peck. Faulkner's *The Sound and the Fury*, its title taken from one of Shakespeare's great tragedies, a great modernist icon and a difficult but profound text on which many a high school student and legions of college English majors have cut their teeth? An embarrassing version starring Yul Brynner as the moral hero Jason Compson (who in the novel is pathetic, misogynistic, unbrotherly, selfish, unvaryingly and self-destructively materialistic, and mean-minded—an unimaginative, supremely comic figure). Faulkner produced six novels labeled masterpieces by literary critics out of the twenty plus he wrote, but the only fictions he constructed that were even moderately successful as film were *Intruder in the Dust* and *The Reivers*. These were not among the six masterpieces. Ernest Hemingway? one of the most popular critically acclaimed American novelists and so well-known he was a media star as well as a skilled writer whose transformational style imprinted itself on so much of the fiction written in the years since 1920? His three great novels *The Sun Also Rises*, *Farewell to Arms*, and *For Whom the Bell Tolls* have yielded not a single film worth ordering from Netflix. James Joyce? Two cinematic versions of

Ulysses, but neither particularly celebrated as of this date. Marcel Proust? *Forgedaboutit, s'il vous plait.*

GIVEN THESE precipitous heights to scale, why does anyone try? Because, of course, they do. There have been four cinematic (or TV) versions to date of *The Great Gatsby*—the current Baz Luhrmann version, a silent version from the '20s just after the novel's publication, the '70s version with Robert Redford (which many current viewers remember, but not particularly favorably), and one television version. Of course, films are narratives with characters, and most novels are narratives with characters. Also, as major film corporations I'm sure know, there is a built-in backlog of potential viewers who have read the book or remember it and want to see its film translation; or, correspondingly, a large number of those who have heard about it and think they should read it and will take the easy way out and just go to a two-hour film instead. But the rule of thumb, with some noteworthy exceptions, remains: the more sophisticated, the more perceptive and well-written the novel, the worse the film. And vice versa. *The Godfather* is a truly great film based on a mediocre novel by a potentially talented writer; this is a significant comparison, since the Coppola film version tells yet another story of failed (and sympathetic) American Dreamers and epic criminals such as Fitzgerald aimed for in *The Great Gatsby*; but Coppola manages to do it cinematically, adding depth with his use of light and dark, paired and subtle images, and powerful, disturbing scenes.

But film-novel translations are pretty much destined to fail for several reasons. One of the key questions asked by the innocent viewer and sometimes by the reviewer is: Is the film a faithful rendition of the novel? But this question begs the essential question: how do you transform a group of words organized into sentences, periods, paragraphs, and chapters to be read and savored over several sittings, into a visual spectacle with a particular rhythm that depends primarily on images? The only way to be "faithful" would be to place a movie camera in front of the text and photograph the pages slowly as they are turned, one by one. As one may suspect, barring an Andy Warhol version, this method is unlikely to produce any enthusiastic responses. After all, this cry for fidelity to the text is not a fair demand; since the two, novel and film, are radically different art forms, perhaps no more alike than a piano sonata and an oil painting, despite surface similarities.

HAVING UTTERED this critical pronunciamento, conscience forces me to concede there have been notable exceptions where fiction has been made into adequate or superb films. Ken Russell's film version of D.H. Lawrence's *Women in Love* is a powerful and imaginative film. Virtually the entire Merchant-Ivory corpus transforming nineteenth and twentieth century fiction into celluloid has been successful. And despite his own lamentable failures in drama, Henry James has had some success in the film versions of *Portrait of a Lady* and *Wings of the Dove*.

Inevitably the text of a novel must be adapted, which in the case of most novels means radically amputated—trimmed of incident and character—since the typical short story of thirty pages offers sufficient narrative drive for a feature film. But a 300-page novel is ten times that length: here *Gatsby* might seem a more appealing subject, since its published versions usually run only 180 pages. One of the passages inevitably excluded from film versions of *Gatsby* is the catalog of Gatsby's guests that Nick records for us on three pages of the novel, a punning comic set piece of American sociology and morality and economic history that is a delight to read, but clearly untranslatable. Consider the following passage of seemingly random character names and socially revealing detail:

"S.B. Whitebait...and the Hammerheads and Beluga the tobacco importer...S.W. Belcher and the Smirkes and the young Quinns, divorced now, and Henry L. Palmetto, who killed himself by jumping in front of a subway train in Times Square."

It is hard to make up for the omission of such a great set piece with overhead CGI views of Manhattan and Long Island or with orgiastic and redundant party pieces and telescoping lenses.

THE OTHER problem a screenwriter-director faces in dealing with great literature is that each choice is subjected by the aficionado (or even the reader) to a heart-rending scrutiny, since it is almost inevitably a change from the text, or—more prominently—from that image carried in the reader's mind and imagination. As a reader and long-term teacher of *The Great Gatsby*, I experienced these near-inevitable disappointments in the Luhrmann film I just saw. Perhaps the most prominent is in the role and placement of Toby Maguire as Nick, for the film Nick is explained as our typical mad narrator, recovering from his experience of Gatsby and his era in a sanatorium in the Midwest, where a doctor prescribes literary therapy. This Nick is a far cry from the voice of the novel, who is mature, sophisticated, distant enough to be admired, sympathetic and involved enough to be credible and moving—but hardly sounding like a compromised individual with a mental or a drinking problem. Fitzgerald's Nick is a lot more like Melville's Ishmael, who escapes the tragedy of the hunt for the White Whale, than a "mad narrator" like Humbert Humbert of *Lolita*. The Luhrmann choice of a mad narrator is more reminiscent of American novels of the 50s and 60s with such equivocal viewpoint characters as Holden Caulfield in *The Catcher in the Rye*, telling us his story from a sanatorium in California, or Randall McMurphy, institutionalized in Kesey's *One Flew Over the Cuckoo's Nest*. Perhaps Luhrmann is thinking of Holden, who is an avowed admirer of Gatsby.

This dislocation of the novelistic narrator Nick also means the truncation of beautiful passages that deftly analyze the deterioration of the American dream, when Nick-Fitzgerald compares Gatsby looking across at Daisy's house to the Dutch sailor "face to face for the last time in history with something commensurate to his capacity for wonder." In the film, we don't see Nick's dissociation from the East and retreat to the Midwest as a moral move but as the last refuge of a destitute alcoholic— even though this latter may track more accurately the trajectory of Fitzgerald's own later years. The morality of Nick's detachment in the novel is underlined by connection to passages and events that are excised from the film: his several key discussions with Jordan Baker about "careless drivers" and his eventual breakup with her because he associates her with the amorality and lack of judgment surrounding Daisy and Tom. Nevertheless, the power of Nick's language is imaginatively underlined on the screen when words issue from his journal and conversation and are highlighted over the visuals, as if in a Brecht play.

EQUALLY PROBLEMATIC are the inevitable incarnations of characters such as Daisy Buchanan and Jay Gatsby himself. Leonardo DiCaprio seems to me a more convincing Gatsby than I might have expected—mature, self-possessed, yet a little uncertain, and very debonair in his pink suit. But his only sense of mystery occurs when he looks pouty or angry, which supposedly is a revelation of depth or disappointment. The problem is that essentially Gatsby is a mysterious, near-contradictory character in the novel, who begins as myth with a few snippets of conversation, may have been related to the Kaiser, is very personable and has a great smile, has a supreme romantic fascination with Daisy that is so intense it transcends personality and character and history, and even has the background of a millionaire whose money comes from bootlegging. It's hard for any single person, let alone an actor in brief moments over the course of two hours, to get this across. It works much better in a fiction that gradually develops these subtle and contradictory details about Gatsby over 180 pages and embeds them in a prose that transforms Gatsby into the ur-American as well as Jesus Christ and a gangster all at once. DiCaprio's first smile at Toby Maguire is ingratiating, but how can that smile, or anyone's smile fully embody the description Nick-Fitzgerald offers of "one of those rare smiles with a quality of eternal reassurance in it, that you may come across four of five times in life....It believed in you as you would like to believe in yourself...Precisely at that point it vanished"? Perhaps Gatsby's attraction is emblemized well in both novel and on screen when Tobey Maguire says meaningfully in farewell to him, "You're worth the whole damn bunch put together."

Daisy is almost an inevitable disappointment in her screen versions, either by Mia Farrow or Carey Mulligan. But I doubt any real woman can embody such a vision that promises all that Daisy promises to Gatsby, is attractive enough to every viewer, and yet is somehow subtly insincere, meretricious, disappointing. At some level, despite its great range and potential, I suspect Fitzgerald's literary vision is simply not cinematic. This is not a fault, but it certainly frustrates Luhrmann. His film does not have the resonance the novel does, in its analysis of the underlying themes of American culture, its bondage to wealth, and its amoral self-deceptions. In fact, Gatsby's parties, a kind of nouveau-riche enactment of the gospel of wealth, are extravaganzas of stage production in the film that are ultimately gaudy and silly, some with oddly anachronistic hip-hop lyrics. Still the scene where Gatsby flaunts around his magnificent mansion showing Daisy his acquisitions and eventually tossing her down elegant shirts is wonderful, so many shirts that it's as if the interior is that of the Ralph Lauren emporium in Manhattan. The demonstration is both exhibitionist and somehow sexy and works on Daisy as it works on the viewer.

DESPITE ITS failures, the film still gets a lot right in powerful sequences: the billowing white curtains that first introduce us to Daisy and Tom and Jordan; the slag heaps of the Valley of Ashes that abut Manhattan and the bedroom communities of East and West Egg that reveal the underside of the American dream of success (along with an allusion to T.S. Eliot's "Waste Land"); the disembodied spectacles of Dr. T. J. Eckleburg that hover over the landscape and punningly suggest a vanished God and appear on the 1925 cover for the novel; the murder of Gatsby as he falls, deluded and unaware, into his San Simeon-like pool, shot by Wilson, who is jealous of the wrong man.

In the end, the current film version functions as a great vehicle to advertise new Gatsby-era fashions and retro diamonds from Tiffany's but tells us very little about Fitzgerald or Daisy or Gatsby or the vanishing American dream.

18. Who *Is* the Genius?
Genius

GENIUS is a movie you're likely to miss, but shouldn't. In our little burg it got two stars out of four, an invitation to skip it, and ran for perhaps one week at the local art theater downtown. It was previewed in advance a number of times, but apparently never made it out of its dim downtown venue and may have been seen by 300 people—perhaps—in a metropolitan area of one million.

You've already gathered it's not a blockbuster, and I'm not arguing it should be the next *Star Wars* or *Jason Bourne*, which is due to come out this summer. Nevertheless, *Genius* has an all-star cast, and you should consider seeing it: Colin Firth, Jude Law, Nicole Kidman, Guy Pearce. You might remember that Pearce played Firth's older brother, the abdicating King of England, in *The King's Speech* six years ago, and was scolded by the soon-to-be King George VI for his lethargy and self-indulgence; whereas here the roles are somewhat reversed, with Pearce's F. Scott Fitzgerald remonstrating with Jude Law's Thomas Wolfe for his dissolute and alcoholic lifestyle, which is threatening his art.

The film begins in a train station with repeated shots of a man's shoes. There is a lot of this sort of deflection, and a care in the movie-making—the avoidance of faces, the sense that details matter, an attention to the mundane, which is somehow also the momentous.

Nevertheless, *Genius* is about a subject dear to my heart, literature—how it's made, what it comes out of. In a direct, focused sense, this subject gets little play in its competing medium of film. The affair between Wolfe and his patroness, his first editor and protector, Aline Bernstein, played by Nicole Kidman, appears to help generate his first great novel, *Look Homeward, Angel*.

And we catch Wolfe just as he's humbly and beguilingly submitting it to Charles Scribner's Sons, publishers, in the person of its primary editor, Maxwell Perkins. A good chunk of the film's first part is taken up by Perkins obsessively reading this manuscript, though he has no apparent pre-warning of its or its author's greatness. We first see him in his office in Manhattan at his desk with his hat on receiving the manuscript; he reads it in this office, his hat still on; he walks to the train, his hat still on, reading the pages as he walks; he sits in the commuter train with his hat still on obsessively looking at the words. He sits at dinner with his hat on at home in Connecticut. We see him in various places around his house with his hat on reading the novel. This is a man who is dedicated to his task and who is clearly absorbed by what he is reading, in some ways indifferent to the mundane world and perhaps certain social niceties. He never takes off his hat for the first two-thirds of the film.

GRADUALLY WE also see Wolfe talking with Perkins, animatedly in conversation with his mistress, and we see Perkins interacting briefly with F. Scott Fitzgerald, whose wife Zelda is in a mental institution and who is down on his economic luck. Perkins unreservedly writes him a check. We also see another Perkins protégé, Ernest Hemingway.

The film's title is ambiguous or teasing about its referent—is the genius Wolfe, about whom fewer contemporary viewers have heard than about Hemingway or Fitzgerald, or is it Perkins? The film title disguises yet further, and amplifies, the ambiguity of its source, Scott Berg's study of Maxwell Perkins, *Editor of Genius*.

SO WE learn that Perkins has a deep and satisfying family and home life, surrounded by a wife and four daughters, while Wolfe never marries and eventually abandons his devoted mistress and first mentor Bernstein. Yet we also see both men, in parallel scenes, rejecting the pleas of their lovers in order to work together on the novel at hand (rejecting stridently in Wolfe's case, mutedly and discreetly in Perkins', as his wife leaves with their daughters for a short road-trip vacation). And Perkins is the full-service editor, as we see him diligently offering his protégé judicious and dramatic reductions in text, along with much praise and encouragement. Text reduction and reshaping was a crucial service Perkins offered Wolfe as an editor, for Wolfe in manuscript was notoriously long in the judgment of many critics, in need of pruning. Some others disagree, having published versions of Wolfe texts that restore the original, far longer manuscript version.

The artists are, by contrast, flamboyant—Fitzgerald with his emotional and financial breakdown, Hemingway with his exuberance and deep-sea fishing, Wolfe with his womanizing and drinking. Perkins is that button-down man who cares deeply about literature, shows little emotion, and keeps his hat on. Presumably his is the steadiness and vision that can add refinement that makes the art accessible and more effective to a wider number of readers.

Wolfe experiences the exuberance of sudden fame, wealth, and critical admiration with his first novel *Look Homeward, Angel*. He is that figure who composes tirelessly on the top of refrigerators, preferring them to desks. He is the Harvard graduate who is finally experiencing literary success (it was rumored that Wolfe had read, or attempted to read, all the volumes in Harvard's Widener library.) This success affects his lifestyle and his writing, as his second novel is far more "exuberant"—or at least abundant—as we see the manuscript of what became *Time and the River* delivered to Scribner's offices in multiple deep boxes, and sheaves of paper tied with string. The project looks and was enormous, about the length of the seven volumes of Proust's *Remembrance of Things Past*; Perkins' editing cut it down to a manageable and commercial length.

Still, in the film, Perkins muses on the role of an editor, who is clearly devoted to creating and improving literature but wonders whether he really produces a greater product or just diminishes and obscures true beauty and greatness. (Along these lines, in the year 2000, Matthew Bruccoli, a Fitzgerald scholar, unearthed and published in its entirety *O Lost*, the original version of *Look Homeward, Angel*, which "marks nothing less than the restoration of a true masterpiece to the literary canon." It is also worth considering the effect Raymond Carver's editor had on his original short stories—for example, truncating one of them to the enigmatic and powerful "Bath," a quintessence of literary minimalism; yet most readers and anthology editors prefer the original, restored, much longer version, "A Small Good Thing.")

WOLFE IS seen in bars and carousing at parties; occasionally Perkins joins him but draws the line when offered a prostitute. However, Perkins does greet Wolfe exuberantly when the writer returns aboard ship from Europe. Perkins not only meets him at the pier, but they also go drinking together, and it is the editor who throws the rock through the window to enter Wolfe's abandoned first apartment, where he had composed his magnum opus.

But it seems inevitable that this friendship, bordering on a family connection, should deteriorate: Wolfe is the son and companion Perkins—father of four daughters—had longed for, Perkins the second father and mentor succeeding Wolfe's own father's early death. Wolfe begins to disregard Perkins' advice, threatens to leave for another publisher, and travels to Hollywood, where, ironically and poignantly, a clearly ruined but firm Fitzgerald gives him pointed advice about how disloyal and pathetic his treatment of Perkins is. This scene itself is a kind of ironic reversal of roles for Guy Pearce, from his character in *The King's Speech*, where he played opposite Colin Firth, who played his younger brother and the future king of England. Here Pearce as Fitzgerald remonstrates with Jude Law as Wolfe, as Firth had remonstrated with Pearce in the earlier film, about his lack of direction and the general dissoluteness of his life.

Wolfe's career and energy dissipating, we see him in a scene collapsing suddenly on the beach. Within weeks, the writer is dead at 37, of what now seems like a strange and inexplicable disease, tuberculosis of the brain.

19. War & Art Part II:
Maudie

A VERY different kind of film from *Dunkirk* is *Maudie*, an indie biopic about a Canadian folk artist, Maud Lewis, which played in only two theaters in town for a week. Like *Dunkirk*, it is based "on a true story." But Maud's life and art are different from our common parables about human existence, or the life of an artist. And so the film is a commentary on the intensity and power of personal vision, dedication to beauty, and the transcendence of loneliness and suffering. A single film can do all that. Maud lived her entire life in a small town in Nova Scotia, and most of her adult life in a small house on its outskirts.

Maud's beginnings were not auspicious. When we first see her (played by Sally Hawkins), she is being deposited as an adult at her aunt's home by her brother, who has sold the family house and can't take care of her any more. She suffers from a partially crippling type of arthritis. Neither of her relatives is sympathetic; her brother is obsessed with money; her aunt never offers anything but criticism. But Maud likes to paint and even goes to a nightclub on the weekend and dances by herself. What gradually emerges is the intensity of her own vision and the subtle and determined ways in which she pursues it. She notices an ad put up by a local near-illiterate fish peddler named Everett Lewis for a live-in cleaning woman and walks several miles relatively slowly but deliberately to apply. This terse and seemingly unemotional housemate, played in powerful understatement by Ethan Hawke, is demanding and grudging, but allows her to decorate with paint surfaces and odd boards around the house and assumes she will sleep in the same bed. Without outrage or intense argument, when Everett begins intercourse, Maud interrupts, suggesting marriage. As in so many modest and great things, she persists and gets her way. She is clever and appealing in appeasing a neighboring customer who complains about some of the fish she was sold, but also accepts Maud's decorated cards as part of the bargain and begins to pay her for them. Though Everett hardly seems thoughtful or romantic, in many scenes he accommodates Maud's disability by pushing her around in a handcart, in idyllic shots surrounded by snow.

MAUD HAS a passion for painting, and we see her painting not only boards and holiday cards, but also her walls and windows, with decorations from nature. (Eventually Maud Lewis painted virtually every surface in her house with birds, flowers, oxen, snowy landscapes—even the stove and the exterior walls; the house and she were such a phenomenon that after her death, contributors from the community rescued it, entire, from dereliction and installed it whole in the regional art museum in Halifax.) We see Maud selling her painted works occasionally outside her house; she charges nickels and dimes, eventually $5. Ultimately she even gets a request for a painting from Vice-President Nixon. Her fame brings her media attention and a film crew to the house. We never hear of any of her art work being sold for much more than $25.

As Maud's aunt ages and gets ill, Maud demands of her husband to visit her only living relative. When he refuses, she walks the miles to town to see her aunt. In a powerful scene, the aunt, a total critic and cynic and actually far more lonely than Maud, acknowledges that Maud is a success—this is the traditional narrative arc of such films, though Maud is far from wealthy. The aunt says that of all the members of her family, Maud is the only one who is happy. Which we now realize is true— despite her disability, her genteel poverty, her frequently distant spouse, she has found materials from life that give her joy and has continued to paint until her death. Such lives deserve recognition.

20. Lateness in Art and Life: A Late Review of *Last Quartet*

THIS FILM foregrounds music in ways that are rarely done in American cinema, though it uses that focus to trace the elaboration of a 4-way intimacy. It's a quartet, not a tercet, so it's not the traditional romantic triangle, but there are three men in various involvements with a single woman, all of them playing classical music together for 25 years as a group designated "The Fugue." This one woman is in various stages and types of love with the three men; however, we don't see a great deal of bedroom antics onscreen—a brief fling by the married man with a much younger woman; a longer affair between the one offspring generated by the two married members of the quartet and the chief violinist. So, the focus is primarily on relationships and music rather than on bedroom acrobatics.

We do learn a certain amount about music, at least for those of us like me who are not experts but merely occasional aficionados. We learn that Beethoven's Opus 131, a very late quartet and one of the pieces the group focuses on during the time covered by the film, is remarkable for having seven movements while the traditional quartet has four. We also learn that the role of second violin Robert Gelbart, played by (Philip Seymour Hoffman), is not simply second fiddle to first violin, but has responsibilities and skills unique to the role, often in counterpoint. However, this explanation comes from the second violinist himself. Juliette, his wife and the violist (Catherine Keener) is often a bit too honest, never quite saying what he wishes she would say. In one scene he abruptly leaves a cab in mid-journey, so devastated by her middling support.

THE CRISIS confronted by this foursome, however, is not essentially romantic; it is the crisis of evolution, aging, and eventual death—one meaning of lateness. Early in the film, the cellist, Peter Mitchell (Christopher Walken), presents the group with, essentially, a genteel ultimatum. He has learned from his physician that he is in the early stages of Parkinson's Disease, and it will eventually and inevitably affect his playing. Not wanting to go out in severe decline, he wants the next concert to be his farewell, and he wants the quartet to progressively incorporate his replacement. As artists, friends, and idiosyncratic personalities, none of the other three is enthusiastic about this decision. The second violin chooses it as an opportunity to press his long-held desire to be first violin, at least occasionally.

We see the four in a variety of settings, in their apartments, in the snow, in cafes, in bed. One powerful climax comes when Gelbart punches out Daniel, the first violinist, for having an affair with his daughter. Presumably, this is for a variety of reasons—that the affair toys with his daughter's affections for an older, accomplished man who is also her mentor, that since it involves three of the principals of the quartet, it assaults the supposed emotional equanimity of the group. Although the assault is also a kind of displaced reaction for the role Juliette has played all along, married to one quarter member, carrying on a variety of not quite clear flirtations or intimacies with the other two male members of the group. Gelbart is too refined to directly confront his wife or even fully articulate to her his dilemma or disappointment, so as the shrinks say, he acts out: he has a one-night stand with his regular female running partner, who is also a flamenco dancer; he physically assaults Daniel.

THERE ARE scenes in a frozen Central Park, scenes among horses in upper New York State, scenes in music classes conducted by Peter. We learn various tidbits that inform both music and life: that all instruments lose their tuning over time, in different ways—a kind of synecdoche for what is happening to the quartet itself, subtly attuned to each other but also falling out of tune, withering with age, seeking near incestuous relationships, engaging in fistfights, having doctrinal disputes over perfectionism v. passion in music. Robert's ode to Daniel about the need for passion in playing music is followed, ironically enough, by Daniel embracing physical passion with Robert and Juliette's daughter. But

Daniel's superior musical skill and perfectionism also hide his loneliness and his privacy. He hides his vulnerability and flaws under a cloak of criticism and "artist's temperament."

Despite tension, rupture, breakup, and violence, the four return to play music and resume their performance of Beethoven's Opus 131 after Peter retires in medias res on stage and is replaced by Nina Lee, who is actually cellist for the Brentano Quartet, the background group playing the music we hear. Supposedly the structure of the film by emotion echoes the emotional structure underlying the seven movements of Beethoven's Opus 131. We also learn that Schubert on his deathbed seems to have requested the playing of this piece.

Juliette may be the emotional center of this quartet/triangle, but she always seems sorrowful, near tears. In one way or another she may be in love with each of her three partners; it's clear she confides regularly in Daniel and hides their confidences from her husband Robert. At some level it may be that the daughter's affair with Daniel is a kind of offer of love from Juliette, though apparently none of those involved is directly aware of this.

At one point, Daniel points out what a key artistic decision it was to become a member of a quartet as opposed to a soloist: playing the same pieces over time with the same people leads to a self-discipline and heightened awareness that can create change as well as develop perfection in art; this can contrast with a variety of random encounters with accompanists and orchestras. Some quartets are nearly eternal, such as the Guarneri Quartet, with its four original players staying together for nearly 45 years. So, this film is an attempt to implicitly examine musical construction and human relationships using an unusual key.

TOWER

Film Collection Reviews, Comparing Genres

21. Across the Genres, from the Mythical West to the Dystopian Future: *A Million Ways to Die in the West,* *Chef,* *Palo Alto,* *Locke,* and *The Rover*

THE FILMS *A Million Ways to Die in the West, Chef, Palo Alto, Locke,* and *The Rover* represent ones I've seen within the last month, and they merit some attention, even if you decide not to see them. But each seems to represent a different genre, or a different tendency in filmmaking, and a different tendency of some creative people to move off in new directions, but most still remain disappointing in some way.

THE TITLE of *A Million Ways to Die in the West* (2014, directed by Seth MacFarlane) seems to encompass the plot; and it's obviously a Western, but the Western, like the dying West, is a dying genre, only it's been dying for a long time. The first American feature film was a Western, *The Great Train Robbery* (1903). At the very beginning of filmmaking, when writers, cameramen, directors, and audiences were still trying to create, delineate, and appreciate this startling new development in technology, it was silent, only ten minutes long, "based on a true story," and photographed in New Jersey, with its spindly birches—not an iconic Western landscape with mountains and deserts. This was some 30 years before the Western became an iconic, mythic form, almost a ritual or sacrament and a mainstay of film narratives for three decades. The West to which it had referred had begun to atrophy soon after the Civil War's end in 1865 and was pretty much a dead issue by 1890, some ten years before its first cinematic version.

But one key element in the Western is nearly always nostalgia—loss and longing. Some of its other constituent narrative and visual elements, which you may recognize from your childhood and the following list, whose items are duly ticked off in *A Million Ways to Die in the West*: long rides across barren spaces on horseback, set against a backdrop of monoliths (often from Arizona's Monument Valley, as if they were scenery dragged out at Western movie-making-time), climactic gunfights (this film has three), a race between a train and horses, sheepherders, Indians, the hero gets the girl. *A Million Ways* parodies all of these, deconstructing them but going far beyond the American revisionist Westerns of the late 1960s (think of *The Wild Bunch*, 1969, *McCabe and Mrs. Miller*, 1971, even *Blazing Saddles*, 1974) into superficial sarcasm and ultimately sophomoric humor—fart jokes and references to fellatio and anal intercourse supposedly are sufficient to replace plot, theme, and, sadly, entertainment.

THE TROUBLE with this brand of humor is that it appears to be thrown in to show how hip the film is, how it doesn't believe any of the myths. Instead it is often irritating, or just juvenile or silly. But it does have an unusual performance by Charlize Theron as the gunslinger's sympathetic (to the hero), yet bitter wife, and Theron has said she was dying to get the role. The film was written, directed by, and stars Seth MacFarlane. Its other noteworthy feature is a series of cameos by various actors, usually placed for their anachronistic value in deconstructing the Western itself—Jamie Foxx as Django in an antiracist killing tucked into the credits, Bill Maher in a comic bit, a figure from *Back to the Future* discovered in a garage, Wes Studi as Cochise.

CHEF (2014, directed by Jon Favreau) is—guess what?—a movie about food and making it. The title suggests a documentary, but we get a quirky independent feature film about an innovative, talented chef trying to save his Los Angeles restaurant's class without alienating his boss, the owner (Dustin Hoffman), for whom profits come first. The first third of the film is exciting, enthusiastic, with collages of the chef buying food, sampling techniques, preparing dishes, and delighting his staff and friends with samples—even seducing his much younger hostess, played by Scarlett Johansson, with a food preparation that subtly borders on the erotic, and makes us wish we were there…to sample the food. He also has an intriguing relationship with his son and ex-wife (who, contrary to type in divorce films, is totally supportive).

And then the film breaks down into renewed (supposedly) gourmet enthusiasm with a new project to purchase a very used food truck in Miami and drive it across country cooking Cuban sandwiches in key locales, such as New Orleans. This plot device fails in two ways at once: the clientele may be enthusiastic, but apparently they are all tasting the same two or three items of cuisine served by the truck—this doesn't mesh with the chef's gourmet enthusiasm and innovation; the city by city locations required by the geography of America (from Florida to California) present no development of theme, character, or even urban character; it's as if we're watching a boring reality show. And the film trails off in predictable ways.

PALO ALTO (2013, directed by Gia Coppola) is an opaquely titled film that was (probably) shown in all of seven theaters across America. Supposedly set in Palo Alto, California (though it was shot in Southern California locales), and based on a collection of short stories with the eponymous title by James Franco, who also acts in a key role, the film is a series of coming-of-age vignettes about a predictably dysfunctional group of teens without genuine adult guidance. Despite the fact that Stanford is just around the corner (though in its own municipality) and that Palo Alto itself is in the center of Silicon Valley, with several certified billionaires lining its city streets, there seems to be no interest in class, sociology, microchips, or even much sense of location. Palo Alto, Spanish for "tall stick," is supposedly derived from a stand of redwoods last seen two centuries ago; no one connected to the film seems to be concerned with this origin either. There are instead a lot of short sticks and immature characters around.

The only thematic pattern or analysis offered is the failure of father figures, including but not limited to the soccer coach/teacher at the local high school, played by Franco, who seduces his teen star and babysitter April. April is the sensitive figure in the film who, sadly and perhaps inevitably, is dismayed when she finds her seduction is part of a player-babysitter seduction succession. There are, surprisingly, few fathers to be found, though supposedly Silicon Valley is overpopulated by successful young males (compared to females). One father invites his son's male friend in, proceeds to offer him pot, and makes a feeble effort at seduction. The central male lead, Teddy, is a troubled (aren't they all troubled? doesn't that seem to be the plot structure and theme function?) teen with a friend, Fred, who keeps making destructive antisocial suggestions that somehow seem attractive; Teddy follows along, but with a quizzical expression that always fails to give full allegiance. Eventually he is arrested for one of their escapades and does community service in a children's library.

LOCKE and *The Rover* offer intelligent and compelling performances by two actors (one British, the other Australian) somehow not fully familiar to American audiences: Tom Hardy and Guy Pearce. Hardy had offered an intensity and unpredictability in his earlier roles as Bain, the mouth-obscuring device villain of mysterious ethnicity and motivation in *The Dark Knight Rises* (2012), following an almost silent, moody performance as a principled and indestructible moonshiner in *Lawless* (2012). Pearce some readers will recognize as having played Edward VIII (George VI's older brother, who abdicated in *The King's Speech*, 2010), but also as having been long ago in *L.A. Confidential* (1997); in between he was a rapacious and epicene federal agent allied against Tom Hardy in *Lawless* as well as the central memory-loss character in *Memento*.

Neither actor is your typical widescreen movie idol, a la Harrison Ford or Brad Pitt. There's an element of tension or painful idiosyncrasy in each, and these two new films highlight this characteristic. *Locke* (2013, directed by Steven Knight) offers us, like so many opaque and distinctive films, a non-explanatory title and a puzzle as its central character, Locke. In fact, this character is its theme and its plot, as we follow along with

Locke, seemingly in real time, as he drives from a giant construction jobsite in Northern England to London along an M highway on a journey that supposedly will transform his life. That's it, that's the whole film. One character, supposedly one scene, but not quite a monologue, because he's a construction executive on his expensive BMW car phone during the whole drive. He's speaking with either his wife, his sons, his construction crew associate, his boss, or an executive from the Chicago-based firm, or a possible girlfriend pregnant and delivering painfully in a London hospital.

IT'S EITHER a bravura performance or a tour-de-force or a terribly ambitious mistake in filming and conception; unfortunately, I vote for the last because of the ways in which these decisions reduce the power and scope of film itself. But we do get to know Locke intimately (perhaps his surname and the film's title are an allusion to the British rational philosopher John Locke or the single-minded attitude he displays in his drive). Locke decides spontaneously or impetuously to abandon a key job and risk his marriage to be by the side of a woman he had a brief coupling with nine months ago.

The portrait that emerges of the man is revealed by his careful responses in phone conversations in that he always seems to be telling the truth and evading emotional ranting: the pregnant woman asks him to tell her he loves her; it would be simple to say so, to comfort her, as he clearly wants to do, but he simply says, in effect, how would he know, he only spent a night with her, a non-committal answer. He is equally rational and deliberate and patient with members of his family and the gradually drunk subordinate who must supervise Europe's "biggest concrete pour" over the next several hours. His other interlocutor is an imagined presence in the back seat of the BMW, his dead father, who never acknowledged him when he was born. This is what used to be called dollar-book Freud; I don't think it has become any more convincing or expensive in the years since and, to me, seems the weakest part of the film.

Though supposedly Locke is in a hurry to reach the side of the woman before she gives birth, we see in the windscreen of his car many other vehicles pass him on the superhighway. His radical decision is apparently not so forthright or certain. But in his conversation with others, he is certain, self-assured. He doesn't seem to want to abandon his wife and sons, but she throws him out "on the phone," as it were. He doesn't want to abandon his job, and we see his expertise and determination in pouring concrete and in chasing down city councilmen and police officers to make sure it arrives on time. He is fired, but there is hardly any doubt he will find a new job. Yet this is hard to take for two hours nonstop. We want what movies generally give us, the intrusion of other characters, other sites, other complications. But *Locke* is unrelenting; Hardy plays well these determined and unrelenting characters.

THE ROVER (2014, directed by David Michôd) is another portrait of a monomaniac, the initially unnamed mysterious character played by Pearce (actually, we learn he is simply "Eric"), but it is also the revelation of a far different world, a world that is so recurrently portrayed in films that, to me at least, it is hardly interesting: the world that is the end of worlds, the post-apocalyptic time of anarchic behavior. And the worlds these display are always dystopic and sadly predictable and uninspired— whether it's *The Road* (2009) or *Elysium* (2013) or even *Planet of the Apes* (1968, 1974, 2001). Some catastrophe, nuclear or geopolitical or ecological, has made the world largely uninhabitable and groups of humans (or apes, in those eponymous films) roam and behave in unpredictable and vaguely threatening ways.

In *The Rover* we are told only that the landscape we first see, of lonely homes and trailers and autos roaming, is "ten years after the collapse," and, given the explicit refusal of many vendors to accept Australian currency, Australia. (America apparently is still stable or unharmed, because vendors will accept American dollars.) In the trailer these scenes are subtitled with the powerful opening lines from Yeats's "The Second Coming"—"things fall apart...the centre cannot hold"— depicting a terrifying, anarchic, and yet poetic world. The landscape is the barren, iconic landscape, as several reviews have pointed out, of the older Westerns I mentioned at the beginning of this review: but, if so, it is a deeply fallen West and its heroic actions are all absurd; eventually, if we stay to the end, we think we understand the reasons for Eric's extreme behavior.

PEARCE SEEMS aging, off-kilter, his face and shirt uncertain or tilted; and we know little of his origins or what he seeks: except that when someone steals his car, he pursues them relentlessly and ruthlessly, though he has at first no weapon. The film is primarily about the landscape he encounters, mostly of aging, oddly paired men, with few women, one a doctor, one an aging grandmother-like figure in a rocker who politely asks Eric his name and offers him an attractive young boy as Eric points a gun at her head. These isolated men live in slowly decaying suburban homes or trailers and cower or sleep in dark rooms, or offer to sell food, and occasionally other human beings for sex. But all is uncertain: What are the rules? What caused the collapse? The Rover, asked repeatedly, refuses to give his name.

There has been some kind of collapse that makes some men horde unappealing food and cower in rooms and steal cars and shoot at each other. At first there is apparently no center, no organization. Yet the outposts we see sell jerry-cans of petrol even if there are no gas stations. And later we are startled to see a long train moving through the barren landscape, even if it occasionally contains soldiers on flatcars manning machine guns. Eric is eventually apprehended by some other soldiers near an abandoned mine and taken to a base and told he will be sent to Sydney, but we don't know for what crime or what fate awaits him. The mystery at the heart of this film and its barren, unpredictably violent tone are what make it distinctive.

22. Potpourri of Year-End Films: *Interstellar, The Theory of Everything, Diplomacy,* and *St. Vincent*

IN THE last month and a half there has been a flurry of films worth seeing, though of varying degrees of excellence and certainly varied in genre and subject.

INTERSTELLAR (directed by Christopher Nolan) is undoubtedly the most touted and advertised of the group and features, as the title suggests, a journey among the stars to a distant planet, since Earth itself is in a death spiral of negative food production, and humanity needs a new home. The best parts of the film, sad to say, are on stable surfaces rather than in the depths of space. But I suspect this is because of the defects of this particular science fiction genre: once launched, the action is limited to a very few characters, and the challenges and outcomes arrive from a predictable and truncated list.

Consider, in this regard, *2001: A Space Odyssey* and *Gravity*. Once in space, the crews of all of these are 5 or 2 and 2, and rapidly diminishing in number for a variety of plot reasons. In *Gravity* it's all about whether the neophyte space astronaut played by Sandra Bullock can deal with her personal demons and somehow land on Earth. This is essentially a one-woman show with stunning visuals, where the technique is the star and the outcome is totally predicted by the title.

Kubrick's classic was far better, though I think there are only three people on Earth who understand the murky ending, where the lone survivor (Dave, played by Keir Dullea) somehow makes it to the distant astronomical site with the echoing obelisk and apparently is transformed into a baby. This is sci-fi crap and mediocre filmmaking; the best part of the film is where Kubrick perfects his art as a satirist (remember *Dr. Strangelove, or How I Learned to Stop Worrying and Love the Bomb*?), when the computer, HAL, essentially a patient, disembodied, gentle (and homicidal psychopathic) voice, goes crazy and Dave is forced to dismantle it and return it to his childhood.

INTERSTELLAR'S starry visuals are often stunning and the landscapes of the distant planet, apparently filmed in New Zealand, are startling, but its plot depends on the theoretical new physics of wormholes and string theory. The scene where the protagonist stares through an interior stellar bookcase locked in space-time into his daughter's bedroom many years ago becomes ultimately tedious and a bit ridiculous. Matthew McConaughey's frantic attempts on Earth to discover NASA's secret program and rescue his family are the film's most compelling elements.

PROBABLY this takes us to *The Theory of Everything* (directed by James Marsh), which is actually about the physicist some of whose theories generate the plot of *Interstellar*: Stephen Hawking. Luckily, this film is not about his theories, but is a love story about his astounding marriage, most of which began in the shadows of his diagnosis, at age 24, of motor neuron disease, which led to the physical limitations of the wheelchair and the computer voice synthesization with which most of us who read newspapers and pay attention to current events are familiar. (But since the film and the review, this noted physicist has died.)

Eddie Redmayne is masterful as Hawking, both as an exuberant, if slightly obstreperous undergraduate at Oxford and graduate student at Cambridge—when he was still healthy—and also later, with his twisted body and comic and inviting leer.

IT IS hard to view the film without being touched by Hawking and his wife (Jane Hawking)'s initial devotion and dedication to addressing the limitations of his illness. The film also traces the gradual deterioration of their relationship as Hawking becomes more interested in his nurse and Jane in her choir director—with Hawking's encouragement. Though this pattern, under the strain of their situation, is predictable, the couple's long years of unity and devotion and three children remain remarkable, especially since Hawking was given an estimate of two more years of life (at 24) when he was diagnosed and lived to an astonishing 76.

Though the film is based on Jane's memoir, occasionally the script must condense and conflate many years; I remained especially puzzled by Hawking's journeying solo to mainland Europe to attend a concert and then requiring emergency medical care (i.e., a plane to fly him home). Other sources make clear that he was attending a continental conference on physics and, after a certain point in his life, has always traveled by private charter jet.

DIPLOMACY (directed by Volker Schlöndorff) is recommended for its minor key and its sidelight on history as well as its paean to often faceless and little-known diplomats who have, as the film would suggest, often saved humanity from great terrors. The film is in French with English subtitles and is essentially a canned drama (a stageplay transferred to film), though the director has made this transformation work. He intersperses the modern acting with black-and-white footage from the actual siege of Paris in the dramatic events of World War II in Europe, and with varied locations across Paris where key events of sabotage are due to take place.

Set in Paris in mid-1944, the film shows us scenes as the Allies advance and the Germans prepare to depart, but first they plan to destroy every major monument in the city—the Opera, the Louvre, the Eiffel Tower, Notre Dame, and all the bridges crossing the Seine—in order to flood the city and crush its civilization, killing and isolating many civilians—and presumably humiliate their long-term enemies, the French.

As the film, and history, have made clear, this was gratuitous violence without much military purpose, but the German general in charge of the city sees it as orders that must be obeyed and cannot be questioned, until he is confronted by Raoul Nordling, a Swedish (hence, neutral) diplomat who knows a secret passageway to the Nazi headquarters and suggests such acts would only cause needless suffering.

The general, seeming at first adamant and unyielding, recognizes the moral power of Nordling's arguments but wants to protect his own family in Germany, threatened with unspeakable treatment should he disobey orders. Given Nordling's skill in argument and suasion and the results, the film is appropriately dedicated to one of director Schlöndorff's friends, the late American diplomat Richard Holbrook, whose negotiations with Slobodan Miloševich helped to end the war in Bosnia. Perhaps intriguingly, Schlöndorff is a longtime personal friend of Angela Merkel, the Chancellor of Germany.

IT'S HARD to leave the review of year-end (last three months') films without mentioning and commending *St. Vincent* (directed by Theodore Melfi), a sleeper and tearjerker, two odd clichés of film response that somehow seem appropriate to this film. Starring in one of his late-reblooming roles, Bill Murray is Vincent, the aging, seemingly cantankerous Vietnam war veteran and neighbor to a youngish single mother with a son in need of a role model. Vincent is always backing his car into his driveway irregularly, progressively damaging his picket fence and fenders, smoking pot, and entertaining at-home visits by his seemingly loving and opinionated whore, played comically and effectively and endearingly by Naomi Watts.

Everyone in this movie seems to be playing against type, from the comic Watts to the relatively serious Murray, to the neighbor played by the now-harassed and relatively realistic and non-outrageous Melissa McCarthy.

BUT IT is her son (Oliver) who steals the show as he gradually begins to appreciate Vincent and his border-challenging behaviors of pot-smoking, foul language, racetrack-betting, and whoring. Even though he is Jewish, the son does a presentation for his Catholic school on a local "saint," and he nominates Vincent and offers a PowerPoint presentation detailing how this seemingly ordinary person qualifies for sainthood.

It's a bravura performance by Jaeden Lieberher, which, even in the rose-colored glasses of satisfying Hollywood endings, rings true, and made me (and others) cry longer than any adult likes to do in public and raised echoes of the respect for the virtue and generosity and decency and suffering in ordinary humans that is a subtheme of James Joyce's *Ulysses* and James Agee's *Let Us Now Praise Famous Men*.

23. A New Trend in Films?
(Essentially *Selma*)

I GO to see many films, as many as I can and still have a life and still be human. My goal is two films a week. That would be 104 films a year, more if you add the few that are relegated to first viewing at home via video or streaming. Serious film reviewers by contrast and for comparison often see 200 to 400 films a year. It has seemed to me lately that more and more films are "factually" "based"—that is, their source or origin or impetus is a biography or history. This would include films this year such as *Selma*, which is both biography and history; or *The Imitation Game* (about Alan Turing, the Enigma coding machine, and the beginnings of computing); or *Big Eyes* (about the artistic couple the Keanes, and how the husband stole most of the glory and his wife's ideas and talent); or *The Theory of Everything* (see review 22); or *American Sniper* (about a returning Iraqi vet, and the emotional challenges he faces). I know many films begin with some kind of subtitle or suggestion or claim, "based on a true story," and that this has some resonance and power and draw for a potential audience.

Yet I think of films as an artistic medium rendering a kind of aesthetic or inventive response to events of human existence, where the "based on" is far more important than the "true story" part. It took a long time for the public and colleges and the intelligentsia to accept the claim that film was an art form. Perhaps the transformative era for me occurred when I was in college (lo, some 50 years ago), when there were no film departments nor film majors nor film schools, but simply film societies: it was under the auspices of these in their various configurations that I became acquainted with the French New Wave in films such as *Hiroshima mon amour* or *Shoot the Piano Player* and where I came to see the films of Chaplin and, later, Keaton as not merely funny and entertaining but thoughtful and perceptive and yes, art. It was under such influence, and others, that the American era of great filmmaking and great directors and film schools began to be built, and led to such films as *Bonnie and Clyde*,

The Godfather, *American Graffiti*, *M*A*S*H*, and many others. You might note that among all these films, almost randomly listed, only *Bonnie and Clyde* might be said to be factually or historically based, though it is far from accurate or historical in its intention or result.

Of course, reality checking (against databases) is helpful and often more accurate or fair than memory. For example, the Academy Award nominees for 2018 (not necessarily the best, or certainly the most representative films) include nine entrees, and three are what might be called fiction films: *Whiplash*, *Boyhood*, and *Birdman*. In 2013, six of the nine were fiction films; in 2011, five were fiction films; in 2004, when there were only five nominees, four; in 1994, three were fiction films; in 1974, all five, one of which was *American Graffiti*. So, apparently there has been this gradually increasing movement away from films created, at least in a sense, out of pure imagination.

ONE CAN try, at least for a little while (a few paragraphs), to sympathize with movie makers. There's this constant demand for films, and this is what they do, and good scripts are so hard to come by, and the average studio-based film is so expensive to make: this is why films gravitate toward "proven trends," often to their own default—why there are so many avatars of *Rocky*; why there are a number of remakes of *The Great Gatsby*, none of them at all great; why *Titanic* gets remade every generation despite the fact that there is basically no plot and we all know how it ends; why "bankable" stars are enlisted to create a salable property. And why a script that comes out of headlines or biography or a known commodity that is based on a true story, like "history," has its appeal. It suggests power and authenticity, or maybe it has the appeal of reality TV, in that it is actually (or reportedly or, with certain qualifications) taken from life. And the outlines and key events of the screenplay are thus presumably already written. But, like all generalizations of half-baked theories, this is grossly distorted and misleading thinking—since, for example, it is no easy task to distill the events of Stephen Hawking's epic, periodically painful and compelling romantic life and theories into a 120-minute film; it is not easy to decide what to include about the background of Martin Luther King's epic battles against Southern (and national) bigotry to achieve the results that are foregrounded in *Selma*; it is not easy to synthesize or summarize the events of Chris Kyle's life from 5 to 39 to make *American Sniper*. To its credit, *American Sniper* is a far more inclusive and challenging film, in dealing with Kyle's changing mindset and absences from home, than the title would imply: it's not just about sitting camouflaged on a rooftop with a spotter and a radio connection picking out particular targets with a high-range rifle.

OF COURSE, mentioning *Rocky* remakes and *The Great Gatsby* and *Titanic* reminds us that a fictional basis is no guarantee of a fundamentally distinguished film. I suppose we could also note in the context of this discussion that Shakespeare, clearly a brand name in drama and excellence, created a number of plays with pre-made plots based in history, such as *Richard III*, *Henry IV*, and so forth. One might add that though Shakespeare may have taken some plots from Plutarch's lives or contemporary British chronicles, he didn't seem much constrained by facts, and he employed great imaginative skill in creating imaginative and psychologically intriguing characters and dialogue for some supposedly known figures of history. Nevertheless, his *King Lear* or *Hamlet*, perhaps mythically based on some dim histories, are far greater plays and characters. I hope it's also clear that I have great respect for the achievements of many of this year's films, especially in terms of acting and script.

Yet the tendency to make increasingly more films based "on a true story" seems problematic and unfortunate to me, a kind of "easy way out." Find a compelling pre-made packet, such as a recent memoir with some kind of cinematic elements, select the key parts, then film it. Don't try to imagine what a compelling or representative character might have done, don't fit background, context, imagery to an imagined plot. The plot is premade in history, just eliminate the confusing elements. Okay. This is a simplistic and superficial critique of the tendency. But I still find great fiction far more compelling than nonfiction.

THEN THERE is the other problem, somewhat artificial, that this tendency creates. The near-obvious, near-inevitable critical question: is the film true to…the true story? Perhaps this is as much, for me at least, a red herring as the critique of films derived from novels: is it true to the book? I would argue that some of the best films based on "material from another medium," such as *The Godfather* or *Shoot the Piano Player* or *Petulia,* are intriguing or powerful because of how they alter the material and transcend it.

Films based on key historical events, such as *Selma,* inevitably raise similar questions, because perhaps they distort history, as if history were such a fixed essence, rather than constantly being reevaluated and rewritten every year—consider the number of books just this last year, on the hundredth anniversary of the beginning of World War I, in 1914. *Selma* has provoked criticism based on its portrait of President Lyndon Johnson, seen in the film as a partial foil for Martin Luther King, its hero. Johnson emerges as a reluctant chief executive, delaying King on his planned civil disobedience to assure voting rights for African Americans in the South, because as Johnson in the film suggests, he has many other things on his political plate.

To the film's credit, this is not a fair account of its portrait of Johnson, who eventually willingly leads a voting rights act through Congress and gives a nationally televised speech assuring the viewer at the end, echoing the civil rights anthem, "We shall overcome." In fact, some of Johnson's best moments in the film come when he sits down in the Oval Office with King's (and the film's) true antagonist, a slimy nasty Governor George Wallace, and uses a variety of encouragement and disparagement, including four-letter words and "good ole' boy" comments, to sway Wallace to be far more flexible and to remind him of his egalitarian roots. Joseph Califano, a former Johnson aide, has come to the President's defense and advised people not to see the film (it's this kind of silliness that some historical films engender) because he maintains Johnson was far more in favor of voting rights than the film portrays him. Perhaps it's telling that the person who would appear today to know most about Lyndon Baines Johnson, Robert Caro, the biographer with four volumes already out on the President's life, has remained mute in this controversy.

The film does some justice to the actual history in reminding us there were three marches across the Edmund Pettus Bridge, neatly increasing the drama and the tension—from the first, where King and the marchers are met with police violence and disperse; to the second, where they are apparently invited by the police parting ways, to march, but King turns around; to the third, where their ranks are swelled by prominent figures from across the U.S. and backed up by uniformed U.S. Army soldiers, and complete their march to Montgomery, the state capitol of Alabama.

Somewhere in its treatment of "history," which is, in this case after all, what we all know or can know, is the murky problem of King's speeches. I realized, as I watched the film, that though the actor's cadences were those of King, none of the speeches seemed particularly memorable or outstanding; then I learned that the director, Ava DuVernay, herself wrote these King speeches, since she was unable to obtain the rights to the ones King actually gave, because Steven Spielberg owns these rights (for a planned film biography of King). To me, that makes the film significantly disappointing, but it is simply one of the inherent problems in filming history.

24. 2½ Summer Films Worth Seeing:
A Most Wanted Man,
Lucy,
and
Begin Again

MY LAST summer film review apparently was a downer for some readers, who concluded I was turned off on the films I saw, and that none of them were worth seeing, which was not my point, but I'll try not to be so opaque in this review of three films that opened recently, and each of which is definitely worth seeing, with some minor reservations about the third: *A Most Wanted Man*, *Lucy*, and *Begin Again*.

FIRST COMES last. *Begin Again* (2013, directed by John Carney), as its title—two 2-syllable, 5-letter words perhaps echoing the two paired characters at its center—suggests, is about that great American—or perhaps human—theme: renewal. Dan Mulligan (Mark Ruffalo) is an alcoholic down-at-his-heels music executive; Gretta (Keira Knightley) is the female accompaniment to an on-the-verge-of-fame rock singer, who has just been romantically abandoned. Their chance encounter as Gretta sings her lugubrious folk dirge with guitar at a Manhattan bar leads to a musical collaboration that reveals hidden depths and possibilities in both of them.

The film's structure suggests how key this encounter is by beginning with it, then looping back through the backgrounds of both Dan and Gretta to explain why the moment is so transformative. Dan is entranced and pitches Gretta with the possibilities of a singing and recording career, even though he has just been fired from the company he helped found and has to borrow the money to pay for their beers. As she sings, solo and lonely and tentatively and unheralded on what is barely a stage, Dan can envisage and we can see full-range accompaniment to her singing with bass, drums, and other instruments: he can see (and hear) how to produce her. He imagines an album based on a series of outdoor Manhattan locales where each song is recorded, without the benefit or encumbrance of studio or civic approval.

THAT'S THE premise, and it's pretty much the story, and we're encouraged to believe it's beneficial for them both. Dan and Gretta collect an enthusiastic near-volunteer group of staff and accompanists and we see them play with the Empire State Building and other iconic Manhattan landmarks as background. We see Gretta charm Dan's rebellious and lonely daughter, and Dan even talk to his ex-wife. We see Gretta's former boyfriend write a new song to entice her back and plead for reunion, after he realizes American stardom and a flaky American mistress don't solve all his problems.

Begin Again has beautiful moments, as in Gretta's instrumentalist friend who supports and accompanies her, as in Dan's now exceedingly successful rapper friend CeeLo Green (Troublegum), who offers him financial and moral support and hugs and comes up with an impromptu rap, duly recorded by his amanuensis, to explain the ideas working in the collaboration. Dan also begins to drink less. The plot arc is a bit predictable, and Ruffalo's alcoholism seems canned, while Knightley's smiles seem ubiquitous and artificial.

But, admirably, the arc startles us by not leading to the romantic juncture of Dan and Gretta. Dan goes back to his ex; Gretta rejects her former boyfriend's entreaties to reunite. The renewal and imagination come in the form of their business success: they don't press the CD or go the corporate route; that route seems to have manipulated and squelched both of them; they make the tracks from the Manhattan collaboration available free on the internet through the push of a button. On the downside, the idea of recording each song free in a different New York locale sounds, for the most part, better as an idea than it plays out as reality. Since they're not making a video, locale doesn't seem very important. We are told by the film that Gretta's songs are indelible, but not all of them are particularly memorable or touching. Of course, this wouldn't be the first time an artist or genius a film displays to us is suggested as producing remarkable or indelible works, while what we see on the screen or hear in the soundtrack is, sadly, very delible. Yet other attentions to the mechanisms and values of the contemporary music business are plausible and convincing.

LUCY (2014) has three stars—Scarlett Johansson, Morgan Freeman, and Luc Besson (the director). And it promotes the idea of using a much greater part of human brain function through a visually stunning, if somewhat clichéd plot. Freeman plays a college professor cum neurologist whose lectures are initially interspersed through the plot introducing Lucy (Johansson), also named after the earliest anthropoid currently known to science, since she will become a transformative figure and transcend, apparently, history, time, and space. According to the professor, humans use only 10% of their brain power, but he speculates they could be induced to use far more, and that this would lead to unsuspected connections we could make in understanding and controlling our environment. This is an exciting idea, as when one of my college roommates told me a distinguished professor had told him you could easily exist on four hours sleep a night. I tried it, but it's one of those ideas that seems to promise great potential but fails somehow or inevitably in execution.

Lucy is at loose ends in Taiwan when she is dragooned by a supposed friend into an international plot involving transportation of a new drug by human mules—it's embedded by surgical procedure in their abdomens. The owners and transporters of the drug—a ruthless Asian crime ring replete with its own gunmen, prisons, surgeons, and international contacts—are in awe of this drug, though they apparently have little concept of what it may do. Lucy's surgery leaks, and she becomes super-drugged, increasing her brain employment percentage exponentially. As the film proceeds we periodically see numbers on the screen, as she moves from 10% to 15% to 20% and eventually to 100%. And thus becomes a superhero capable of, eventually, anything: she defeats all her captors with a single gun. We have seen this in films before, executed by supposed martial arts heroes, but it's sadly the cinematic exposition of a kind of deification, though such a god is one few of us would worship for very long. Lucy shoots perhaps seven antagonists in a room simultaneously; she stops martial arts figures in mid-air or midstride simply via an act of will. She communicates with the professor, halfway around the world in Paris, over Skype and his phone and every electronic device known to a hotel room simply by thinking about it.

THE VISUAL effects of Lucy's powers are, of course, stunning in terms of action film effects. We also see computerized visuals of what is supposedly going on in her brain in terms of stellar fireworks and smoke and various simulations. Some of her reflections apparently transport her back to the beginning of human existence, where she meets Lucy, her anthropoid ape ancestor, and touches fingers. The modern Lucy is also great at high-speed car chases through Paris, against traffic and over pedestrian walkways, though as she explains to her cop-protector-guide from whom she's appropriated the car, she's never driven before.

Lucy introduces us to that idealized world where thought not only leads to action but can be transformed directly into action, and of course it's good that Lucy's on the side of humanity rather than....But as her brain usage approaches 100% and she's "winning," it's also clear that she's exhausting her capacity and will die within 24 hours of her initial transformation. As this apocalypse approaches, she is gradually slinking-transforming into a glassy black computer amassing the information she's intuited and appropriated, until she dissolves, like a figure from *The Wizard of Oz*, into just a pile of clothes and vanishes, leaving the professor holding what's left of her: an index drive. *Lucy* is all concept, all action, all fantasy, and quite a trip. The 10% of brain use is not merely *not* a scientific theory, however, according to an article in *Scientific American*, it is kind of a modern urban myth, mistakenly attributed to Albert Einstein or William James; nevertheless, Morgan Freeman is authoritative, and Scarlett Johansson is beautiful and somehow warm, and we believe this myth at least for as long as the film lasts.

THE BEST of these summer three and the one not to miss is *A Most Wanted Man* (2014, directed by Anton Corbijn), with Philip Seymour Hoffman, touted as his final film. It is a spy thriller, though neither of the

James Bond type nor of the Jason Bourne type: there is minimal violence and no shooting. It is derived from a recent novel by John Le Carré, who has renewed his metier, famous from *Tinker Tailor Soldier Spy* and *The Spy Who Came in from the Cold* (TV serial and films and novels from the 60s and 70s), in the milieu of the snooping against modern international Islamic terrorists. As always in Le Carré, the human transgression counts more than the spy craft, and the climax is in minor defeat and suffering. The central figure is often sad and compromised in some way and mistreated by the spy bureaucracy. But the situation still makes for powerful drama, as it does in *A Most Wanted Man*. The title is a kind of pun since it apparently refers to two men, Gunter (Hoffman), the German off-the-books counterespionage agent, and Dr. Faisal Abdullah, an Arab in Germany publicly supporting cooperation and charitable operations, but some of whose solicited funds always seem to disappear elsewhere. Both of these figures are wanted by others—by the American CIA chief Martha Sullivan (Robin Wright), by the German police and official spy apparatus, by various agents.

Gunther is a non-acknowledged agent allowed by the German authorities to stretch or break certain laws, but they regularly contact him suddenly on the street or in various restaurants to suggest they want to end or take over his activities. He's on a short leash after an embarrassing failure in Beirut several years back. Gunther is in nearly every scene, speaking English with a German accent (a film convention to avoid interminable subtitles), chain smoking, and often seen with a drink in his hand, though never drunk. He schmoozes with spymasters, with Ms. Sullivan, with his colleagues, talks to informers, encourages, nudges, demands, to get what he wants. He's a bit rumpled, rarely uses physical force, seems reliable, but not always powerful or totally assured. The one scene where Gunther throws a punch—unrelated to any form of espionage—is to protect an unknown woman in a bar being physically mistreated by her boyfriend. This kind of odd footnote gives Gunther humanity and credibility. The last time we saw this lumpy, overweight actor throw a punch, was at a fellow musician in *Late Quartet* who had seduced his daughter (and perhaps his wife).

THOUGH GUNTHER is the linchpin character, there is a brilliant ensemble cast of suspicious and ambiguous characters: Rachel McAdams as the German lawyer for the Chechen, who is thrown into a car with a mask over her head and told by Gunther she's essentially a social worker for terrorists; Willem Dafoe as a German banker for dubious depositors who is forced against his will to cooperate with the German spies; and of course Robin Wright as the American connection, an embassy or CIA figure who alternately seems sympathetic and distanced from Gunther and finally betrays him. But betrayal is one of the currencies of the film: the young informer Gunther meets irregularly and furtively in various public places around Hamburg—a cigarette shop, a ferry—turns out to be Abdullah's turncoat son.

What Gunther wants is Abdullah, but Gunther is not heartless. The way to Abdullah is through a suspected terrorist, Issa Karpov, a Chechen illegally in the country and with few friends, but Gunther recognizes he is essentially harmless and, through intermediaries, gains his cooperation to get to the bigger fish. The fish metaphor, cliché as it may be, is expanded in a grand scene at the film's mini-climax, where Gunther must present his case in a stunning conference room in Berlin to about 20 interlocutors. This is a brilliant scene in its distance from the daily machinations and its demands on Gunther and in its evasive corporate atmosphere. Gunther explains why he seeks Abdullah and won't give him up: you catch the small fish to get to the barracuda, the barracuda to get to the shark….One of those present professes to be baffled by the fishing metaphor (hard to believe he's sincere, since we in the audience are way ahead of it). Gunther is asked what he seeks to achieve by his operation; he replies, "Perhaps to make the world a little better place," an unarguable if vague nostrum which, it turns out, he had elicited days earlier from Martha, and he smirks to her as he says it. Neither really knows where the operation leads; ultimate purpose seems to elude everyone. And the dubious morality and reality of seemingly attractive, but vague, clichés is doubly questioned by this echo and the smirk.

Of course, we don't know where Abdullah leads, and when the sharks of international intelligence, with the CIA's knowing nod, swoop in to steal Abdullah from Gunther, who is ready to turn him, we don't know where they will take him or what they will do to him. We don't know what's beyond the shark. The film ends anticlimactically, with Gunther in a rage at his upstaging, and he drives a little distance and parks his car. Has he gone back to work on another case? Is he abandoning his job entirely? We don't know.

These may not be the greatest films of the season or even of the year, but they do represent distinct, different, and imaginative worlds and offer strong performances by some of cinema's gifted actors.

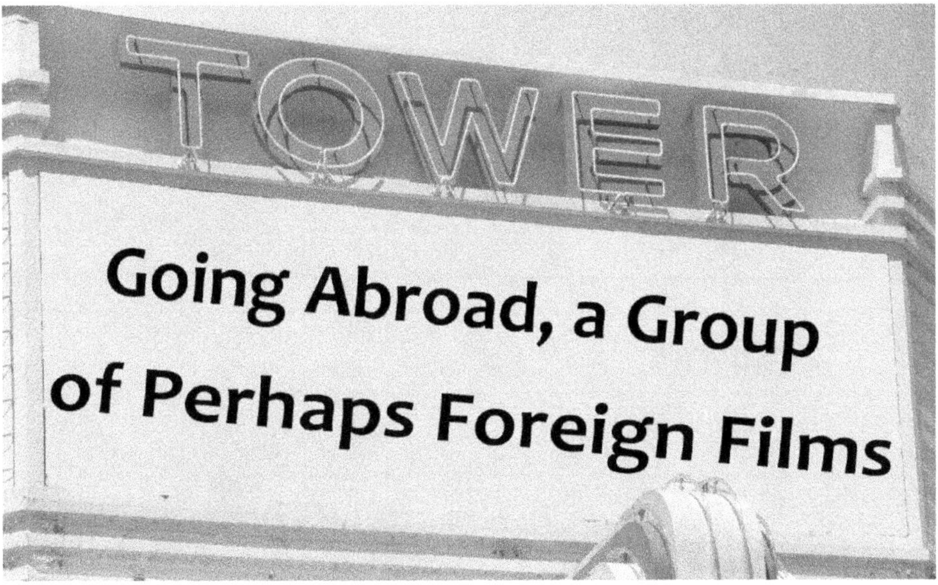
TOWER
Going Abroad, a Group
of Perhaps Foreign Films

25. A German Huckleberry Finn?
Barbara

MOST OF you, if you're like me, will not have previously seen or have heard of *Barbara* (2012, directed by Christian Petzold), a film I saw recently at an art house (or what used to be called an art house, but is now a multiplex with an occasional "art house" film) in Berkeley near the University of California. It's one of those small, simple, slight, unprepossessing but troubling films that don't make it into the list of the same 15 films that are spread around every multiplex in your medium-size city and involve vampires or cars or teenagers or space travel or apocalypse or Presidents.

Not that these big-screen, big-budget films aren't worthwhile, but to me it seems, having come of (film) age in the 60s, that the availability of and interest in small films has markedly diminished. Now I barely write that sentence and think of all those far more adept at technology and knowledgeable than I who will point out that there is a cornucopia of cineart available through legal and illegal downloads on the web and on indie cable channels and so forth. But I still bet in your intimate circle of friends you'll be lucky to find one who's even heard of the recent West German import *Barbara*. And now I'll actually talk about the film itself, which is well worth seeing if you don't want to be part of an audience jumping up and cheering or feeling good, or going to a chick flick with predictable lines and plotlines.

This film, in German with English subtitles, is about the life of a woman doctor in East Germany during the 1980s while the country was still divided by Cold War establishments and tensions, and East Germany was a police state where a high percentage of citizens were spied on by the Stasi. The title is ambiguously nondirective, suggesting very little about the film's topic or course. Of course, *Barbara* is a character study, but it probes with some sympathy and surprising conclusions the inner life of those whose inner life was constantly watched by the state. If you want to enjoy the surprises the film has to offer, stop reading here.

WE FIRST see Barbara (Nina Hoss), from outside as she arrives for her first day of work at a rural hospital. It's an open question whether we ever really see her from inside. She is an attractive, aging blonde, with her hair pulled back, who rarely smiles, but smokes nervously—perhaps to avoid what she is feeling, perhaps to delay whatever it is she must view next. She is being observed by two male onlookers, Dr. Andre Reiser (Ronald Zehrfeld) and Klaus Schutz (Rainer Bock), who we later learn is with the state police, from a distant window as they discuss what they know of her. She is under suspicion immediately because she has been rusticated here after a prison sentence due to anti-state activities, presumably an attempt to escape East Germany. Nevertheless, as the film develops we discover she is a competent, even compassionate and thoughtful, doctor who gets about town on a bike and rejects most offers and overtures from Andre, her colleague and superior. We realize eventually that he too has been rusticated after some kind of medical failure, but also appears to have made a pact with the Stasi. So, his interest in Barbara isn't disinterested or even romantic; yet this actor generates genuine sympathy and concern. He offers Barbara rides in his car and gives her a Turgenev novel and seems to want more.

Stella (Jasna Fritzi Bauer), a new patient, arrives, brought in resisting by a cadre of state police: she is a young girl sentenced to a work camp who has tried to escape but is also ill. Barbara diagnoses her meningitis almost instantaneously, supervises her treatment, and becomes a kind of substitute mother. The most powerful scenes are where she reads at night to the patient from *The Adventures of Huckleberry Finn*. Such an eruption of classic great literature from a foreign society is not only a mark of the film's culture and idiosyncrasy, but a clue to its intentions: Barbara and her charge are implicitly compared to Huck and Jim, refugees temporarily from a hostile society but doomed by geography (of the Mississippi River) and history to return. Like Jim, Stella must be returned to her plantation. Escape seems possible via water, but the outcomes are uncertain.

As we follow Barbara we learn she makes clandestine connections with other dissidents and receives contraband currency. The police obviously suspect her and regularly visit her apartment at impromptu moments. We watch as Klaus sits dispassionately and a bit bored in a chair while his several underlings search the premises and a matron comes in donning rubber gloves to complete a search of Barbara's body cavities: use your imagination, because the film doesn't quite go there. There is a kind of bureaucratic brutality here, but it is extremely understated. It's part of a ritual. We reevaluate meaning as characters and events recur. Later we see Andre attend to Klaus' wife at home, where she is apparently suffering from a terminal illness, and Klaus himself seems stricken in a chair outside. When we add this to all the previous scenes, everyone in the film appears simply as an emotionally drained human being dealing with a common tragedy of existence.

THE FILM is often compared to another recent film, far more critical about the Stasi, *The Lives of Others*. The Stasi was, after all, the all-pervasive, seemingly all-inquiring, state police authority. Sometime after the wall came down, ordinary East Germans were able to consult their own Stasi files, only to discover that the principal informant against or on them might be a wife or a husband or a best friend. But *Barbara* also tries to take into account that somehow real, non-heroic people, continued to live their lives; as Nina Hoss, who plays Barbara, has commented about her experience, "If you talk to the people who lived in the GDR…they say, 'we loved, we had kids, the grass was green, I had a wonderful childhood.'" The GDR also brought us Angela Merkel, the democratically elected Chancellor of Germany, now ready to embark on her last four years in office, the longest surviving leader in a Europe in turmoil. Perhaps this formerly emotionally distant and discarded society has something to offer.

The atmosphere of a Hitchcock thriller or a Bergman psychological study is reinvoked by the vulnerability of the protagonist cycling along country roads, by her nervous cigarette smoking, by the several mysterious scenes in a windswept locale surmounted by a cross and rock where she buries certain contraband, in this case German currency from the West. Though we expect harm to come to her or for there to be some dramatic confrontation, the climax comes on the night when Barbara had planned to escape to the West via water: as a wet-suited agent like a God or avenging angel rises from the sea to help her escape and raises one finger to indicate he can't take her and Stella both. Barbara gives up her chance for a new life in the West and lets the girl go.

Barbara has made the decision to remain in the East, and it forces us at the end to reconfigure the film. She has decided for the potential lover Andre, who, though he may be in league with the Stasi, is fundamentally decent. She has decided for a life of work, where she can offer something, as opposed to an apparently pampered existence in the West where her clearly wealthy lover tells her she won't have to work; he seems loving and attractive but appears only episodically and doesn't offer her much. Andre, however, whom she kisses once, is far more appealing and seems to know her at some depth, even if he may be in league with her apparent enemies. Oddly enough, she has decided for humanity rather than ideology.

26. Philosophy, Ambiguity, and Humor: *Le Week-end*

FEW FILMS every year transcend the obvious categories and expected strategies and actually try to address the problems real people encounter in their lives, as opposed to a remake of *Spider Man*, another battle of World War II, or an inventive heist with many guns and the "heroes" escaping. *Le Week-end* (2013, directed by Roger Michell) does transcend these tired dramas. And its French-English title suggests both its location and its mixed heritage of British reticence and boredom and French liberation and sexual possibility. Even the title suggests the confusion of its heritage, since it is a legitimate phrase in France, incorporating an English phrase that is more clear and more concise and more direct than whatever French might cook up—but also a bit comic, casual, and offbeat, and maybe puzzling.

The film is set in Paris as an aging British couple, Meg and Nick Burrows (played by Lindsay Duncan and Jim Broadbent), arrive to take a brief holiday before returning to their marriage and their daily lives. As it continues, we discover that their two children are (almost) out of the house, that Nick has been involuntarily retired (read "fired") from his job as a college Philosophy professor, that they are both comfortable and bored with each other—though for much of the film we are never sure quite which condition predominates. Nick suspects Meg of a longtime secret affair, Meg threatens to have a drink around the corner with an attractive male, and the word divorce is mentioned.

But there is also the atmosphere of liberation from quotidian restraints, of experimentation, even of joy in spontaneity. Meg rejects the first hotel they arrive at, where they had stayed on their honeymoon, because of its beige interior and moves them to an elegant suite at a clearly more prestigious and expensive Parisian hotel. At one restaurant meal, Meg orders Nick to wait for her outside with their coats, then descends to the cellar and rummages around mysteriously until she finds an exit to the street, where they both rejoin and then joyously or furtively escape, apparently, the bill. Until this point, there is no indication that they are in financial difficulty. The hunt for the first restaurant is an echo of tourist's joy in the profusion of Parisian choices, and in the quick-cut shots declaring "too touristy," "too empty."

BUT FOR much of the film it's not entirely clear what difficulty Meg and Nick are in, and that is part of its mystery and its charm. Each member of the couple is beset by reservations and critiques of the other, not so uncommon as their marriage has lengthened into years and they contemplate the ends of their careers and eventually their lives. At times they seem radically incompatible and dissatisfied with each other, but frequently they are as chummy as well-adjusted thieves.

Another restaurant scene shows the wife experiencing supreme joy in her carefully chosen soup as she tries it, then shares a taste with her husband. She also offers him a kind of treat, taking him to the Paris cemetery where some of his heroes are buried, and he pays homage at a grave, an impressive large and understated flat stone block bearing the name "Beckett." Even though the husband's academic specialty is philosophy, Beckett is a Nobel prizewinner in Literature who sets the tone, presumably, for this film's catalog of human suffering and ills, where the participants, like Sisyphus, keep carrying on. The mixture of boredom, disaffection, humor, and comedy is captured in a number of iconic near-stills, like the one of the couple, as in a Toulouse-Lautrec painting, seated at a restaurant table side by side facing the camera, she with a man's hat, each looking a bit inebriated, a bit lost, a bit isolated.

There are some great dialogue exchanges, some comic sequences, and a great sense of ambiguity and, perhaps, love. One memorable and revelatory exchange: "You make my blood boil like nobody else!" "Sign of a deep connection."

A KEY set of climaxes in the film comes as the Burrows respond to an impromptu invitation to a party from Morgan, a former Cambridge classmate of the husband (played by Jeff Goldblum as a successful American writer and public intellectual at his insouciant, self-involved, slightly silly, best), who apparently has no financial problems, but lives in an elegant Parisian home with his now-pregnant second wife. Morgan seems the center of a literary-philosophical salon, and his party is attended by successful thinkers in a variety of fields, in contrast to the Burrows. But at the party Nick and Meg retreat into their own separate, isolated states, wandering apart and apparently both lonely and depressed after their painful series of revelations to each other during the weekend.

Meg is at first alone on a balcony staring forlornly into the beautiful Paris skyline, though she is soon joined by a younger man who shows some romantic interest and invites her to a drink at a bar around the corner.

Nick wanders around the large house, as his wife had earlier wandered in the restaurant basement, and finds his way to the room of Morgan's alienated teenage son. Professor and adolescent, like lover and wife, find something in common in their mutual alienations and satisfactions—and this is one of the film's more remarkable scenes. Nick admits he, unlike the French, is both incapable of and disinterested in adultery. His revelations are accompanied on his earphones and the soundtrack by a voice-over of Bob Dylan's "How does it feel to be on your own?"

The dinner at the center of the party issues in four remarkable speeches, each of which plays off the others: they are given by Morgan and wife and then by Nick and Meg. The pregnant wife pays tribute to her husband, who then pays tribute to his friend and former colleague Nick. Nick, however, offers a truthful and depressing self-analysis, saying he is bankrupt, has been fired, and his wife has been asked to meet a younger man and she should.

Finally, in a comic sequence, the couple are barred from their hotel room because the husband has trashed one elegant wall with clippings and pin-ups and because their credit card is maxed out and they can't afford the bill. The room clerk reminds them that he holds their passports locked in his safe, but essentially offers no resolution. So, as in the earlier financial crisis, they escape. Their only hope is Morgan, who meets them at a bar and offers to let them stay at his house until he sorts this out.

As the film ends they escape their mutual troubles by dancing in line to a retro tune, spontaneous, happy, and a bit beyond the borders of the assured or probable—and in echo of Godard's much earlier film *Bande à part* (1964).

THERE IS a kind of liberation in despair, honesty, and breaking—mildly—the law. There is also joy. Whether they will divorce or acknowledge their mutual affection and dependence, we don't know; whether Morgan will tire of his adulation up close we can't say; how they will retrieve their passports and emerge unscathed is open to question.

27. Adultery, Viager, and Their Discontents:
My Old Lady

THE FRENCH are reputed to say, perhaps thinking of *Madame Bovary*, that "without adultery there is no novel." And of course adultery, both practical and literary, is not limited to the French. But there is a French setting for the film *My Old Lady* (2014), about, among other things, adultery. Israel Horowitz, after 18 years, has made a filmed version of his play, and taken it from its apartment confines and entrances and exits out onto the streets of Paris. And his work's take on adultery is neither romantic nor particularly sympathetic and, in that way, is refreshing without quite being puritanical.

Mathias "Jim" Gold (Kevin Kline) is shown tentatively and a bit awkwardly moving about Paris looking for an address, which proves to be in the newly fashionable Marais district. He enters an attractive, older building; when no one responds to his ring, he searches the rooms on several floors until he eventually finds Mathilde Girard, an old woman played by Maggie Smith, almost cowering in a corner apartment. As the American explains to the British resident of the French building, he has newly inherited the property, the only asset his father left him after dying. But the rental is actually a *viager*. This derives from the arcane, remarkable, and nearly whimsical French practice explained several times and in several ways in the film—a kind of reverse mortgage, to assure aging residents of both income and domicile, and to offer investors and prospective home owners a potential bargain (if the resident dies earlier rather than later); but essentially it is a kind of lottery based on age and mortality estimates and human (dis)honesty, as many aging residents disguise their age and infirmity in order to secure better terms.

All is not what it seems, and neither character in this initial encounter can be fully trusted. Jim will use his own devices to sustain his economic viability—mostly disreputable and deplorable. We also discover that the "tenant" harbors a subtenant, Chloe (Kristin Scott Thomas), Mathilde's resident daughter.

THESE OPENING complications set the stage for the film's two subjects: the viager, the one we think we don't understand, and the adultery, the one we think we do. Thomas has been in several classic films with adultery themes, though she has made many other genres: she is the dying adulterous lover in *The English Patient*, worth sacrificing a civilization for; in *The Horse Whisperer* her character falls in love with, but never consummates the adulterous attraction to the horse whisperer who helps to rescue her daughter from emotional and physical pain; in *Random Hearts*, she is, along with Harrison Ford, a mutual victim of adultery after the adultery is discovered following the simultaneous deaths of their spouses. Perhaps in the latter case, we might be tempted to remark, without adultery there is no film. Kristin Scott Thomas, a resilient and recurrent actress in both English and French films, has recently appeared in *Tomb Raider* as the new guardian of the young Lara; though seemingly trustworthy and staid, the film ends with the suggestion that she is duplicitous.

In *My Old Lady*, Chloe eventually reveals to Matthias that she was present when her mother had clandestine meetings with his father, and that she was complicit in the deception her mother practiced on her own father. Matthias also, apparently observing no social limits in his quest to retake the viager property, stalks Chloe and discovers she is having an affair with a married colleague. He blackmails her, threatening discovery. His relationship with Chloe seems adversarial and tense, but they are actually sharing, since they, as their discussions reveal, are both victims of adultery, even though Mathilde, the sole living participant in the adultery, remembers it with intensity and affection, regarding it as a high point in her life.

THE ATTRACTIONS of adultery, its historic literary and popular appeal, are evident in fictions as disparate as *The Scarlet Letter*, *The English Patient*, *Anna Karenina*, and *The Great Gatsby*, to mention but a few in a long tradition. These fictions generally offer great sympathy and understanding for the lovers, almost universal distaste for the absent mates, and a variety of climaxes. Virtually all these literary and cinematic adulteries provide beautiful settings for their affairs, as does *My Old Lady* with Paris: among others, there are some beautiful shots of Jim walking lonely by the Seine and encountering a woman singing opera, with whom he performs a duet. But despite its romantic setting, the film explores and implies the suffering adultery has caused in absent mates and offspring.

MATHILDE'S SELF-deception is confronted in a variety of ways. She had always thought that Jim's mother was unaware, or at least untouched by the adultery, which occurred in a foreign land, and that she had died after an illness. But the film reveals Jim's and his mother's troubled family history, seen as a result of his father's infidelity. The film's ending revelation undercuts its Parisian-beautiful-romantic-nostalgic view of adultery. It strikes Mathilde like a powerful blow. It brings Chloe and Jim close enough together that they become lovers. In fact, the film is about the loneliness of the three central characters, who have lived alone for long parts of their lives and, despite personal charm and wit and intelligence, are clearly unhappy. In the grand tradition of American movie happy endings, the dilemmas of both the viager and the pain of loneliness are solved by Jim and Chloe's love affair and Mathilde's offer to forgive rent and provide Jim a place to stay. It's a bit too neat, given the strong emotions the imaginative plot has set in play: homeless, unemployed recovering alcoholics rarely find such an easy solution to their problems.

Nevertheless, *My Old Lady* offers key coy, comic, and powerful performances by its three principals. Comedy, tragedy, and pathos are intermixed, as when we hear a gun explode in Jim's upstairs room and think he has committed suicide in alcoholic stupor, but has only shot a stuffed boar, relic of Chloe's adulterous, absent father.

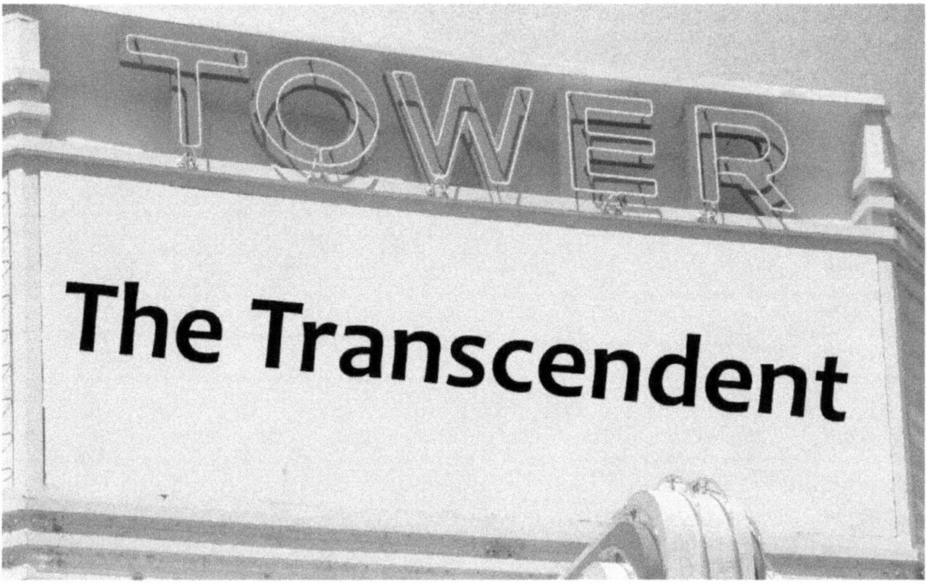
TOWER
The Transcendent

28. Hidden Tiger, Crouching Theology: *Life of Pi*

GO SEE *Life of Pi*. That's the short version. Unfortunately, though I am a fan of movies and movie reviews, I am caught in a conundrum or an oxymoron or some kind of Rubik's Cube of intellectual difficulty in that: I love seeing movies, I love knowing about them, I love the series of surprises that a great or even mediocre moviemaker throws at me, I love sitting through the four to ten previews or, as a friend of mine so anachronistically called them, "trailers" that precede virtually every movie I see.

And yet, I despise knowing "sound bites" about a movie that spoil its surprises or its best moments, so that you have seen them or read about them before you actually see them in their natural narrative context, where they have added bite; but in which their bites have been defanged because you have been warned. So, I will try to disclose as little of plot or emotional surprise as I can in this review but it's a near-impossible task not to disclose some, and still offer any comment of worth. Some of you may want to take the first sentence at face value and take the risk, and go see the film, then come back and read the rest that follows.

You probably already know *Life of Pi* is based on a prize-winning novel or at least that it is a story of a boy at sea in a boat with a Bengal tiger. That much is fairly true, and its visualization, in Ang Lee's 3D version, is entrancing and spectacular. And yet there is so much more. The more will, inevitably, frustrate you, because you want to see the boy at sea with the beast, and how he manages it and what happens and what it all means. The more keeps interrupting and delaying that compelling central story. For there is a frame narrative of the Indian boy-become Canadian middle-aged man, living as a professor of philosophy in Montreal and played by Irrfan Khan, the same actor who some viewers will recognize played the near-suicidal, uncomfortably acculturated Indian patient a few seasons ago in the excellent HBO series *In Treatment*.

The frame story is, comparatively, visually boring, and mostly predictable in several ways, and yet clearly it provides the key commentary for the central conflict. And it explores two vast human problems, the problem of identity and the problem of divinity, presumably interwoven, for the narrator asserts his own story proves God, and the narrator is in youth a serial devotee of three major religions who wants no conflict between them, presumably a non-discriminating pantheist. And so we may see God, somehow, in the tiger, cleverly named Richard Parker, and undoubtedly in the miraculous whale (already in many of the previews). This theme, perhaps the most challenging in the film, is felt in the magical and mystical beauty of the whale vaulting the boat in the middle of the night and in the series of plagues and manna from heaven that visit the two sojourners, but it isn't stressed much after the beginning.

The quandary of identity is seen also in the viewpoint of the narrator and his listener, a budding novelist—for the speaker is Indian, the listener American, the setting Canadian, his own name apparently Greek—based on the irrational and endless number *pi*, whose digits he is seen scribbling on blackboards in his youth to prevent being teased as "pissing," a derogatory Anglicization of his French given name "Piscine," derived from his father, a swimmer's, love for a pool in Paris. There are many mysteries beneath this seeming cross between *Castaway Robinson Crusoe* and *Huckleberry Finn*. Only here the antagonist is a beast without a voice but with a personality, not a volleyball, nor an escaped slave, nor a servant Friday. All of these present the dilemma of how to deal with human identity on its own, and what it all means.

Index

About the Author

A RETIRED English professor, Jonathan Price has taught courses in American and British literature, composition, and contemporary film, both in California and abroad, including Fulbright awards to Italy and Portugal. Most of the film reviews here first appeared in the weblog "Moristotle & Co." Professor Price has also published—with co-authors—a text on writing under time pressure and another on grammar. In addition to this collection of his film reviews, he is currently seeking a mainstream publisher for the memoir of his Fulbright teaching fellowships.

www.ingramcontent.com/pod-product-compliance
Lightning Source LLC
Chambersburg PA
CBHW052010090426
42741CB00008B/1629

* 9 7 8 0 6 9 2 1 6 5 3 7 9 *